RETRO
GAME DEV

C64 EDITION VOLUME 2

DEREK MORRIS

Be you. The world will adjust.

TABLE OF CONTENTS

Introduction 1

- About This Book 1
- Assumed Knowledge 2
- Suggested Learning Process 2

PART I: GET THE PARTY STARTED 3

Chapter 1: Setup 4

- Toolchain 4
- Run Test 8

Chapter 2: Key Concepts 12

- Registers 12
- Macros and Subroutines 13
- Labels, Constants, and Variables 16
- Indexing 17

Chapter 3: Debugging and Profiling 20

- Print to Screen 20
- Profiling 21
- C64 Debugger 23

Chapter 4: Mind If I Interrupt? 25

- Default IRQ 26
- IRQ with Wedge 28
- Multiple Raster IRQ's 30
- Faster IRQ's 35
- Sprite Multiplexing 40

PART II: LET'S MAKE A BEACH BAR GAME....45

Chapter 5: Wait... What? 46
- How to Play 46

Chapter 6: Billy the Barman.............................51
- SpritePad 51
- Player Sprite..53
- Movement and Animation 55

Chapter 7: Jamaica Mon 60
- CharPad 60
- Display a Background.................................62
- Screen Switching..63

Chapter 8: Things That Go Bump...................67
- Collision Points...67
- Collision Detection and Response 69

Chapter 9: I Need a Drink.................................73
- Variable Arrays 73
- Customers 74
- Walking State..76
- Waiting State...78
- Drinking State...80

Chapter 10: Sun Worship..................................82
- Variable Arrays 82
- Beachgoers 83
- Walking State..85
- Waiting State...87

- Lying State 88

Chapter 11: A Bit Nippy..**91**
- Interrupts 91
- Movement 92
- Collisions 94

Chapter 12: Let Me Hear Ya......................................**96**
- SID Files..96
- SID Player...98
- Game Music and Sfx.....................................99

Chapter 13: That's a Wrap.......................................**101**
- Gameflow 101
- HUD 102
- Memory Usage..105

PART III: REFERENCE.............................. **109**

Chapter 14: Library Code.......................... **110**
- libInput..111
- libMath 111
- libRasterIRQ...118
- libScreen...120
- libSound 130
- libSprite..132
- libUtility..138

Credits **141**

Introduction

Welcome to RetroGameDev C64 Edition Volume 2.

About This Book

This book is for those who wish to further their game creation skills for the Commodore 64 and learn some of the more advanced features the computer offers.

The response to the first volume has been amazing and I thank all of you for embracing the concept to provide a simple yet effective approach to learning a difficult subject. The involvement in the forum, the awesome mini-game mods, and even some published games based on the code library have far exceeded expectations.

The idea behind the first volume was to provide an abstracted library code framework in order that the assembly code details didn't muddy the game development concepts presented. This worked well and will continue here. However, this time as requested, the library code is fully commented and a handy reference section has been added to the end of this book.

Also, rather than two mini-games there is an in-depth look into the creation of a larger multi-screen game pushing further toward what a released product might look like.

I invite everyone to take the Beach Bar game and either expand upon it or use the concepts presented to make your own totally new game. The code is completely royalty free!

Furthermore, feel free to share your game development journey at retrogamedev.com/forum or ask any questions relating to this book and I'll do my very best to answer.

Let's keep these retro systems alive!

Assumed Knowledge

The information in this volume 2 book builds upon the first volume and is not intended as a replacement. Therefore some fundamental concepts from volume 1 are skipped and assumed to be understood in order to follow along with the code explanations. These are:

- Number bases and uses.
- A basic introduction to C64 hardware.
- Fundamental 6502 assembly language explanations.
- How to run .prg files in an emulator or on hardware.

Suggested Learning Process

To get the most from this book I suggest the following steps:

- Download the book assets.
- Run some of the pre-built prg's (Commodore program files) in an emulator, on the C64 Mini/Maxi, the Mega65, or on an original Commodore 64/128.
- Follow through the book trying the experiments and heeding the warnings.

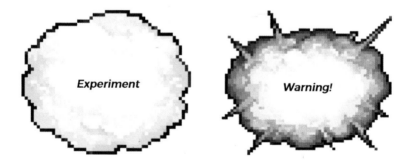

Experiment

Warning!

- Study the supplied code base using the Library Code chapter as reference.

Have fun!

PART I: GET THE PARTY STARTED

Chapter 1: Setup

A Microsoft Windows 10 environment is assumed but other operating systems can also be configured for development. (See retrogamedev.com/forum for more information).

Toolchain

- Download and extract the book assets from retrogamedev.com/downloads.

The tools and installers are in **Tools**

The **.code-workspace** files are in **Chapters\Chapter***

The **.spd**, **.bin**, **.ctm**, **.sid** files are in **Chapters\Content**

- Install the Java runtime from **Tools\Java\ JavaSetup8u281.exe**.
- Install Visual Studio Code from **Tools\VSCode\ VSCodeUserSetup-x64-1.52.1.exe**.
- Open Visual Studio Code, select **Extensions** (1), search for **kick** (2), and install the **Kick Assembler (C64) for Visual Studio Code** extension by **Paul Hocker** (3).

- Check **File->Auto Save** (1).

- Select the **gear icon** (1) on the Kick Assembler extension, then **Extension Settings** and open the **User** settings tab.

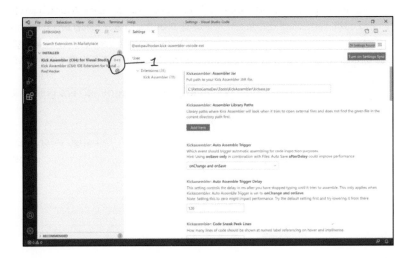

- Fill in your own Kick Assembler extension paths: (these may differ from the images below depending on where the files have been extracted to)

  o Kickassembler

  Kickassembler: Assembler Jar
  Full path to your Kick Assembler JAR file.

  C:\RetroGameDev\Tools\KickAssembler\kickass.jar

  o C64 Debugger

  Kickassembler: Debugger Runtime
  Full path to your debugger runtime.

  C:\RetroGameDev\Tools\C64DebugGUI\C64DebuggerGUI.exe

  o VICE Emulator

  Kickassembler: Emulator Runtime
  Full path to your emulator runtime.

  C:\RetroGameDev\Tools\WinVICE\x64sc.exe

  o Java Runtime

  Kickassembler: Java Runtime
  Full path to your Java runtime.

  C:\Program Files (x86)\Java\jre1.8.0_281\bin\java.exe

- Open **Tools\WinVICE\x64sc.exe**.

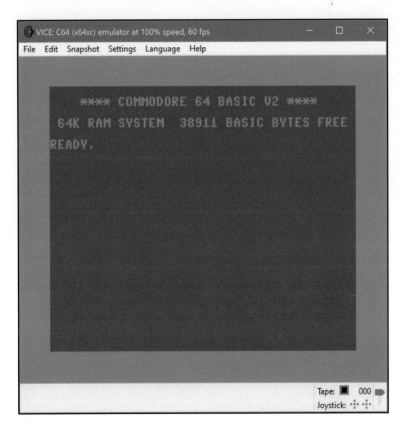

On the **Settings** menu:

- Check **Sound settings->Sound playback, Drive settings->True drive emulation,** and **Save settings on exit.**
- Uncheck **Settings->Confirm quitting VICE.**
- Select **C64 model settings...->C64 NTSC** (to match the images in this book, PAL also works).
- Select **Joystick settings->Joystick settings...** and set **Joystick #2** to **Keyset A,** then choose **Configure Keyset A** to configure up/down/left/right/fire.

Run Test

- Open **Ch1.code-workspace** in **Visual Studio Code**.

This is a simple program to clear the screen, set the screen color, then go around in an infinite game loop.

A link to the same library code files has been added to each chapter workspace using **File->Add Folder to Workspace...**

Therefore library code file changes are reflected in all chapters. If this behavior is not required then duplicate the library code and link to the copy instead.

Changing shared
library code files
affects all
chapters

BasicUpstart is a Kick Assembler built in macro that inserts a short BASIC program at the specified memory location $0801 (the default start location of a C64 program when entering the **RUN** command in BASIC). This executes a **SYS** command to run the machine code starting at the **gameMainInit** label.

The **#import** line tells the assembler to include the library code (at $0810 which is after the BASIC program) to make the macros and subroutines available for use.

The screen is cleared and set to yellow using library macros before entering the gameMainUpdate infinite loop.

The gameMainUpdate loop waits for the display scanline to reach number 250 before looping back around. Doing this locks the display framerate to 50fps (PAL) or 60 fps(NTSC).

There are 2 ways of assembling and running the programs:

- Press **F6** to assemble and run in the VICE emulator.

- Press **Shift-F6** to assemble and run in the C64 Debugger.

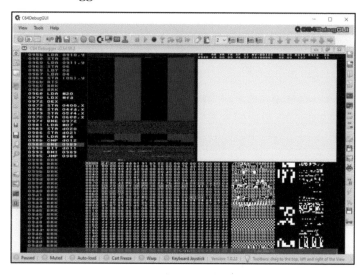

If the debugger doesn't work correctly, try right clicking on the **Visual Studio Code** shortcut, set **Properties->Advanced->Run As Administrator**, then close everything and run again.

When assembling and running a program, the file that contains the **BasicUpstart** must be highlighted (**gameMain.asm** (1) in each chapter unless otherwise stated).

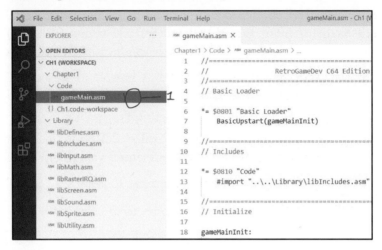

Pressing **F6** or **Shift-F6** on one of the other game or library code files will only assemble that selected file and will not run correctly (this usually exits to a BASIC **READY** prompt).

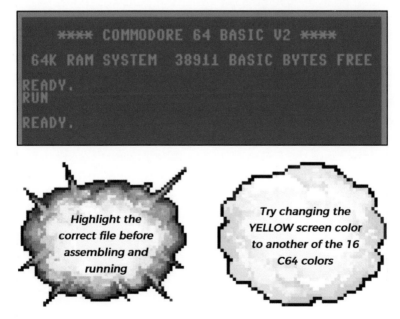

Highlight the correct file before assembling and running

Try changing the YELLOW screen color to another of the 16 C64 colors

Chapter 2: Key Concepts

- Open **Ch2.code-workspace** in **Visual Studio Code**.

It's important that a few key concepts are clear before we begin in order to facilitate further explanations.

Registers

The 6502 has some built-in memory locations called registers that are used as temporary work areas and to store the results of instructions. They are internal to the processor and don't have a memory address, so are identified by their names.

Three of these used often are the A (Accumulator), X, and Y registers. They are 8-bits (1 byte) in size. The A register is often used to perform calculations with, and the X and Y registers are used to copy memory, count, or index into memory.

The 6502 cannot copy a byte from one memory address to another directly. It has to go through an internal register. Here a value is copied from one memory location ($FB) to another ($FC) going through the A register using 2 instructions.

gameMain.asm

```
// Copy a byte from one memory location to another
lda $FB // (l)oa(d) the (a)ccumulator with the value in $FB
sta $FC // (st)ore the value in the (a)ccumulator to $FC
```

Other hardware such as the graphics and audio chips also contain their own registers to control them, and these are mapped into the 6502's memory address space. To command one of these chips to do something, it's as simple as copying bytes of data into these memory locations.

Macros and Subroutines

Macros and subroutines are a way of writing code blocks that can be re-used and therefore provide a modular codebase.

It's very easy to get into a spaghetti code situation with assembly language! Taking the time to be neat and tidy can save a lot of debugging down the road.

The assembler takes each macro call and replaces it with a copy of the macro's code. So even though we'll refer to calling macros, they aren't technically 'called' at runtime.

A subroutine however, has only one copy of the code called at runtime with the assembly **jsr** instruction. Code flow redirects into the subroutine, then returns back to the memory location after the call using the assembly **rts** instruction.

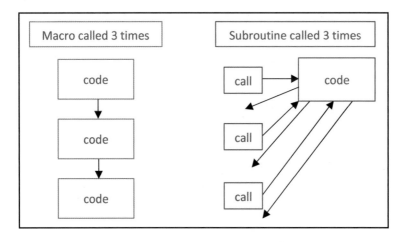

Therefore, macros generally use more code space than subroutines but execute quicker because they don't have the overhead of the **jsr** and **rts** instructions.

Here's a simple macro that provides a re-usable method to set the screen background color. The naming conventions used for clarity are 'filename_purpose_parametertypes(parameters)'.

gameMain.asm

```
// Set the background color
.macro GAMEMAIN_SETBACKGROUNDCOLOR_V(bColor)
{
    lda #bColor // bColor -> A
    sta BGCOL0  // A -> background color register
}
```

The parameter types are **V = value** and **A = address**. However, that's just the naming convention. The thing that determines if a parameter is used correctly is the **#** symbol after the assembly instruction that uses it. **#** means treat the number as a value, the absence of **#** means treat the number as a memory address.

For example, if we pass in **3** for **bColor** and omit the **#** after the **lda** instruction, then it would use the value stored in the $0003 memory location rather than the number 3 (cyan).

A good sanity check is _V = use #, _A = don't use #.

So this macro copies the color value into the A register, then copies the number in the A register to the **BGCOL0** register (which is the memory mapped graphics chip background color register defined in the libDefines.asm file).

'#' = use value
directly,
'no #' = use value
from address

Another convention used is to prefix the parameter names with **b** for a byte (8-bit) or **w** for a word (16-bit).

Next is a subroutine to set the screen border color. As this is a subroutine and not a macro, it needs to be called with a **jsr** assembly instruction and must have an **rts** at the end to return to the calling location.

gameMain.asm

```
// Set the border color
gameMainSetBorderColorGreen:
{
    lda #GREEN  // GREEN (5) -> A
    sta EXTCOL  // A -> border color register
    rts         // Return from subroutine
}
```

The restriction with subroutines is that they can't have parameters (hence why this example has been hardcoded to GREEN).

A compromise between macros and subroutines is to wrap a subroutine within a macro (_S used for a wrapped subroutine).

gameMain.asm

```
// Set the border color
.macro GAMEMAIN_SETBORDERCOLOR_S_V(bColor)
{
    lda #bColor                       // bColor -> A
    sta ZeroPage1                     // A -> ZeroPage1
    jsr gameMainSetBorderColor        // Jump to subroutine
}

gameMainSetBorderColor:
{
    lda ZeroPage1  // ZeroPage1 -> A
    sta EXTCOL     // A -> border color register
    rts            // Return from subroutine
}
```

The parameters are temporarily stored to memory locations in the macro before the subroutine is called. Then the subroutine reads the parameters back from the memory locations.

This would be especially memory efficient if the subroutine was large and called many times because although the macro portion would be duplicated each time it's called, the subroutine wouldn't.

Labels, Constants, and Variables

Labels are names given to constants, memory addresses, and registers using the **.label** assembly directive. The convention used here is FULLCAPITALS for registers and CapitalFirstLetters for the others.

libDefines.asm

```
.label Space        = 32
.label ZeroPage1    = $02
.label BGCOL0       = $D021
```

The other type of labels used are names given to the current area of memory to jump to with a **jsr, jmp**, or one of the branch instructions. They have a : at the end of the name and are most commonly used to identify subroutines.

gameMain.asm

```
gameMainUpdate:
    LIBSCREEN_WAIT_V(250)   // Wait for scanline 250
    jmp gameMainUpdate      // Jump back, infinite loop
```

The **.const** assembly directive is used in the same way as **.label** for constants, memory addresses and registers except that its scope is only for the current code file.

libMath.asm

```
.const MathRandomMax = 64
```

Variables are allocated using the **.byte** or **.word** assembly directives. The area of memory is allocated at the current program memory location. For example, if you had a variable before a subroutine, then the variable's memory address would precede the subroutine's memory address and vice versa.

libMath.asm

```
bMathRandomCurrent1: .byte 0
```

The zero page memory area (addresses $02->$FF) are also used and these are predefined in the libDefines.asm file.

libDefines.asm

```
.label ZeroPage1 = $02
. . .
```

Don't allocate variables with **.byte** or **.word** directly in the middle of code that will be run (e.g. in the middle of a subroutine), as the data will be interpreted as machine code instructions and will most likely crash the program. Allocating before or after a subroutine or macro is fine as that will be outside of the program code flow.

Don't allocate
variables in the
program flow

Indexing

The X and Y registers on the 6502 can be used to index into memory. Think of them like arrays in a higher level language such as C or Java.

Here the value **8** is stored into the A register and the value **3** into the X register. Then the value in the A register (**8**) is stored into the memory location **$FE ($FB + 3)**.

gameMain.asm

```
// Put the number 8 in memory location $FE
lda #8 // (l)oa(d) the (a)ccumulator with the value 8
ldx #3 // (l)oa(d) the x register with the value 3
sta $FB,x // (st)ore the value in A to $FE
```

Try loading different values to A,X,Y and storing them to BGCOL0 and EXTCOL

- Press **F6** to assemble and run in the VICE emulator.

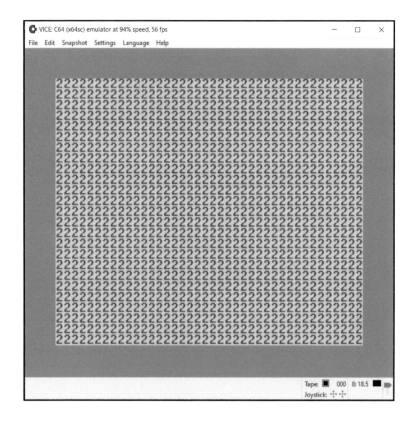

- Press **Shift-F6** to assemble and run in the C64 Debugger.

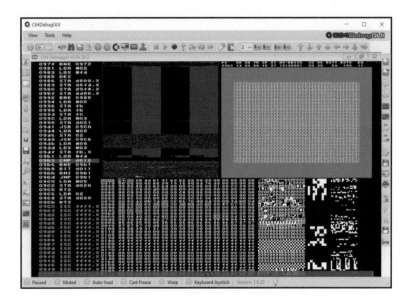

Chapter 3: Debugging and Profiling

- Open **Ch3.code-workspace** in **Visual Studio Code**.

When developing a game there are a number of tools and methods used to help track down bugs and find code that causes gameplay slowdowns. We take a look here at some quick and simple methods of debugging and profiling and also begin to use the C64 Debugger tool.

Print to Screen

The library macros **LIBSCREEN_DEBUG8BIT_VVA** and **LIBSCREEN_DEBUG16BIT_VVA** display the current value of a byte or word (i.e. 1 or 2 memory locations).

The **LIBSCREEN_DRAWTEXT_VVA** macro can also be used to print a null terminated string to give variables an on-screen identifier.

The first 2 parameters are the x (0-39) and y (0-24) screen character positions to print at, and the 3rd parameter is the address of the variable or text.

gameMain.asm

```
// Draw byte variable text
LIBSCREEN_DRAWTEXT_VVA(1, 5, bVariableText)
// Draw byte variable value
LIBSCREEN_DEBUG8BIT_VVA(18, 5, bVariable)
. . .
// Draw word variable text
LIBSCREEN_DRAWTEXT_VVA(1, 7, wVariableText)
// Draw word variable value
LIBSCREEN_DEBUG16BIT_VVA(18, 7, wVariable)
```

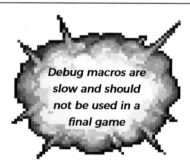

Debug macros are slow and should not be used in a final game

Profiling

A simple way to profile how long a section of code takes to execute is to change the screen border color.

We begin by waiting for a particular scanline each frame to synchronize the screen refresh rate to 50Hz (PAL) or 60Hz (NTSC). This is so our game code runs at a stable frame rate. Without synchronization the game loop would run as fast as possible and its speed would change depending on how much code was executed.

chapter3.asm
```
LIBSCREEN_WAIT_V(250)              // Wait for scanline 250
LIBSCREEN_SETBORDERCOLOR_V(RED)// Start a profiling bar
```

Usually the scanline number used to wait on is around 250 (the bottom of the visible character screen) so that any code affecting the screen can be run in the off screen area. This prevents screen tearing which is when the screen is updated while it's still drawing.

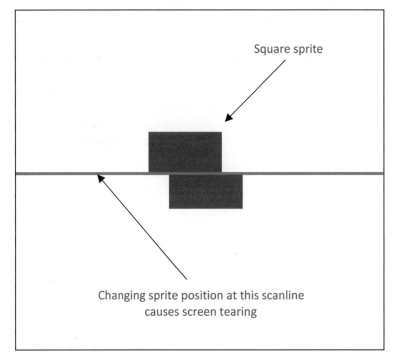

Square sprite

Changing sprite position at this scanline
causes screen tearing

The border color is changed around sections of code to show its location (relative to the frame update) and duration.

- Press **F6** to assemble and run in the VICE emulator.

There are also LIBSCREEN_PROFILESTART and END macros available that simply increment and decrement the current border color.

All code needs to run in a single frame update to avoid slowdown

C64 Debugger

The C64 Debugger is a full-featured debugging tool used to analyze all aspects of the Commodore 64 internals at runtime. We only require a tiny proportion of its capabilities and you are encouraged to explore further by reading the manual.

We also use the C64 Debug GUI which is a wrapper for the C64 Debugger that adds toolbars. It's not a necessity but helps if you prefer icons over keyboard shortcuts.

- Click to the left of the **SETBORDERCOLOR** macro to add a breakpoint.

```
● 47    .break
  48        LIBSCREEN_SETBORDERCOLOR_V(RED)              // Start a profiling bar
```

- Press **Shift-F6** to assemble and run in the C64 Debugger.

After a short delay, code execution halts on the first assembly instruction of the LIBSCREEN_SETBORDERCOLOR_V macro.

- Press **Ctrl-Shift-F3** to switch to the source code view.
- Press **F11** or click **Run** (1) to continue (This runs a complete frame and stops again at the breakpoint).
- Press **F10** or click **Step** (2) to step through the assembly code instructions one by one.

Notice the 6502 CPU registers change as you step through the code (3).

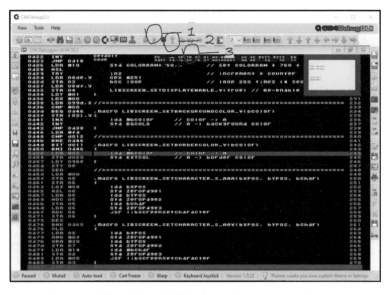

Note that a quirk of the C64 Debug GUI means that you may need to click a toolbar view on the left pane before the keyboard shortcuts will work.

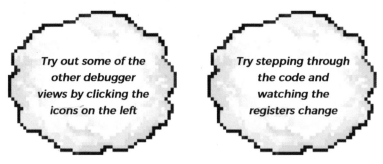

Try out some of the other debugger views by clicking the icons on the left

Try stepping through the code and watching the registers change

Chapter 4: Mind If I Interrupt?

- Open **Ch4.code-workspace** in **Visual Studio Code**.

An interrupt on the 6510 processor occurs when a signal is sent from an external chip to either the **IRQ** (Interrupt ReQuest) pin (1) or the **NMI** (Non-Maskable Interrupt) pin (2).

```
                  6510
    0 in ▭ 1           40 ▯ RES
    RDY  ▭ 2           39 ▯ ◊ 2 out
    IRQ  ▭ 3   —1      38 ▯ R/W
    NMI  ▭ 4   —2      37 ▯ D 0
    AEC  ▭ 5           36 ▯ D 1
    VCC  ▭ 6           35 ▯ D 2
    A 0  ▭ 7           34 ▯ D 3
    A 1  ▭ 8           33 ▯ D 4
    A 2  ▭ 9           32 ▯ D 5
    A 3  ▭ 10          31 ▯ D 6
    A 4  ▭ 11          30 ▯ D 7
    A 5  ▭ 12          29 ▯ P 0
    A 6  ▭ 13          28 ▯ P 1
    A 7  ▭ 14          27 ▯ P 2
    A 8  ▭ 15          26 ▯ P 3
    A 9  ▭ 16          25 ▯ P 4
    A 10 ▭ 17          24 ▯ P 5
    A 11 ▭ 18          23 ▯ A 15
    A 12 ▭ 19          22 ▯ A 14
    A 13 ▭ 20          21 ▯ GND
```

The 6510 will pause its current task, perform a different task, then return to what it was doing previously. This is not multiprocessing as the 6510 can only process a single instruction at a time.

The difference between the two interrupt types is that all IRQ's can be switched off and on by using the **sei** (SEt Interrupt) and **cli** (CLear Interrupt) instructions, but NMI's cannot (at least officially, there are workarounds). They also look at different memory addresses for the interrupt routine to call (also called interrupt vectors). The interrupt vectors are $FFFE-$FFFF for an IRQ and $FFFA-$FFFB for an NMI.

A benefit of interrupts is that code can be run at a specific time without stalling to wait for an event to occur. E.g. run 60 times per second on a timer, or run every frame on a particular raster line (another word for scanline).

For this book we only require Raster IRQ's (i.e. generated by the VIC-II graphics chip when a specific raster line has been reached). However, the following information is still applicable for IRQ's generated from other signals such as a timer.

Default IRQ

When an IRQ signal is generated, the 6510 will:

- Complete the current instruction.
- Save the Program Counter (PC) and Status register to the stack.
- Handle the IRQ routine.

Then, when an **rti** instruction is encountered, the 6510 will:

- Restore the PC and status register from the stack.
- Continue with the instruction where it left off.

The IRQ routine is handled with a ...

- (1) **jmp($FFFE)** - an indirect jump where $FFFE-$FFFF contains $48 and $FF (little endian) so jumps to ...
- (2) **$FF48** - kernal interrupt prep routine that saves the A, X and Y registers to the stack, then does a ...
- (3) **jmp($0314)** - an indirect jump where $0314-$0315 contains $31 and $EA (little endian) so jumps to ...
- (4) **$EA31** - kernal interrupt routine that maintains the clock, scans the keyboard, blinks the cursor, performs a few other functions, restores the A, X and Y registers from the stack, and executes an **rti** instruction.

Default IRQ

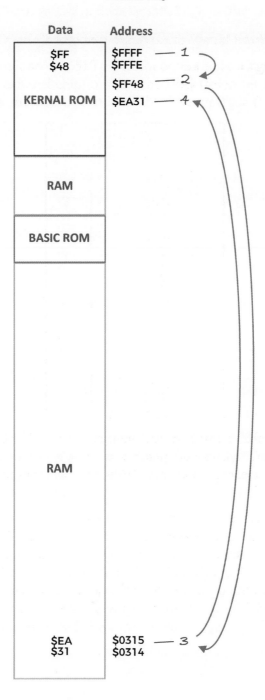

Data	Address	
$FF	$FFFF	— 1
$48	$FFFE	
	$FF48	— 2
KERNAL ROM	$EA31	— 4
RAM		
BASIC ROM		
RAM		
$EA	$0315	— 3
$31	$0314	

IRQ with Wedge

The designers of the interrupt system created it in such a way that it uses two indirect jumps rather than hardcoding the memory addresses.

The first indirect jump via $FFFE-$FFFF is done so that if ever the kernal ROM routine memory locations changed in an update, backwards compatibility would be maintained by simply changing the jump address in ROM.

The second indirect jump via $0314-0315 is in RAM and is placed there to allow the insertion of a custom IRQ routine into the IRQ code flow (also known as a wedge).

In order to wedge a custom IRQ routine we need to:

- Replace the values in $0314-$0315 with our own interrupt routine memory address.
- Jmp to the $EA31 kernal interrupt routine at the end of our own interrupt routine.

The updated IRQ routine with a wedge is handled with a ...

- (1) **jmp($FFFE)** - an indirect jump where $FFFE-$FFFF contains $48 and $FF (little endian) so jumps to ...
- (2) **$FF48** - kernal interrupt prep routine that saves the A, X and Y registers to the stack, then does a ...
- (3) **jmp($0314)** - an indirect jump where $0314-$0315 contains our own interrupt routine memory address so jumps to ...
- (4) Our interrupt routine which will then jump to ...
- (5) **$EA31** - kernal interrupt routine that maintains the clock, scans the keyboard, blinks the cursor, performs a few other functions, restores the A, X and Y registers from the stack, and executes an **rti** instruction.

IRQ with Wedge

Data	Address

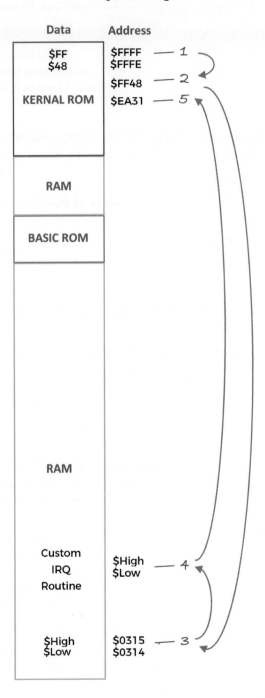

$FF $FFFF   — 1
$48 $FFFE

        $FF48   — 2

KERNAL ROM $EA31 — 5

RAM

BASIC ROM

RAM

Custom
IRQ $High   — 4
Routine $Low

$High $0315   — 3
$Low $0314

Multiple Raster IRQ's

When using raster IRQ's, it's sometimes desirable to run multiple custom IRQ routines each frame.

An example of this would be to split the screen between bitmap mode and character mode as used in some adventure games.

In order to do this, the IRQ's raster line and custom IRQ routine memory address are changed at the end of each custom IRQ routine therefore forming a chain.

The last one of the frame points back to the first so that the chain can be executed again on the next frame.

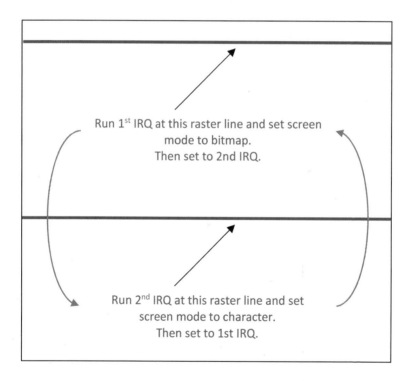

Run 1ˢᵗ IRQ at this raster line and set screen mode to bitmap.
Then set to 2nd IRQ.

Run 2ⁿᵈ IRQ at this raster line and set screen mode to character.
Then set to 1st IRQ.

- Start with the **gameMain1.asm** file.

We first clear the screen and initialize the IRQ system with the scanline and memory address for the first custom IRQ routine using the LIBRASTERIRQ_INIT_VAV macro. This starts the raster IRQ signal happening each frame.

The contents of the IRQ interrupt vector $FFFE-$FFFF are drawn using the debug macros. (Note these values are displayed as decimal so 72 = $48 and 255 = $FF).

gameMain1.asm

```
gameMainInit:
    // Clear the screen
    LIBUTILITY_SET1000_AV(SCREENRAM, Space)
    // Initialize irq
    LIBRASTERIRQ_INIT_VAV(Irq1Scanline, gameMainIRQ1,IrqFast)
    // Draw IRQ vector low text
    LIBSCREEN_DRAWTEXT_VVA(5, 0, irqVectorLowText)
    // Draw IRQ vector low byte
    LIBSCREEN_DEBUG8BIT_VVA(30, 0, $FFFE)
    // Draw IRQ vector high text
    LIBSCREEN_DRAWTEXT_VVA(5, 1, irqVectorHighText)
    // Draw IRQ vector high byte
    LIBSCREEN_DEBUG8BIT_VVA(30, 1, $FFFF)
```

The main game loop constantly sets the screen color to blue and loops around. This makes the screen color blue whenever interrupt code is not running.

gameMain1.asm

```
gameMainUpdate:
    LIBSCREEN_SETSCREENCOLOR_V(BLUE)
    jmp gameMainUpdate // Jump back, infinite loop
```

Each IRQ routine is encased in the LIBRASTERIRQ_START and END macros.

The first IRQ routine sets the screen color to green, waits for some time (equivalent to a few scanlines), then sets the scanline and IRQ address to the next IRQ routine using the LIBRASTERIRQ_SET_VAV macro.

gameMain1.asm

```
gameMainIRQ1:
    LIBRASTERIRQ_START_V(IrqFast)        // Start the irq
    LIBSCREEN_SETSCREENCOLOR_V(GREEN)    // Set the screen color
    LIBUTILITY_WAITLOOP_V(50)            // Wait for a while
    // Point to 2nd irq
    LIBRASTERIRQ_SET_VAV(Irq2Scanline, gameMainIRQ2, IrqFast)
    LIBSCREEN_SETSCREENCOLOR_V(WHITE)    // Set the screen color
    LIBRASTERIRQ_END_V(IrqFast)          // End the irq
```

By setting the screen color to white just before exiting the IRQ routine, white will display on screen until code control passes back to the main game loop where the screen color is set back to blue. This enables us to see how long the ROM code at $EA31 takes to execute.

The second IRQ routine only differs in the screen color it sets and that it sets the scanline and IRQ address back to the first IRQ.

gameMain1.asm

```
gameMainIRQ2:
    LIBRASTERIRQ_START_V(IrqFast)        // Start the irq
    LIBSCREEN_SETSCREENCOLOR_V(RED)      // Set the screen color
    LIBUTILITY_WAITLOOP_V(50)            // Wait for a while
    // Point to 1st irq
    LIBRASTERIRQ_SET_VAV(Irq1Scanline, gameMainIRQ1, IrqFast)
    LIBSCREEN_SETSCREENCOLOR_V(WHITE)    // Set the screen color
    LIBRASTERIRQ_END_V(IrqFast)          // End the irq
```

The green and red bars have been artificially lengthened by using the LIBUTILITY_WAITLOOP_V macro to be able to see the color bars, so the ROM code (white bar) actually takes many times longer to execute than our custom IRQ code.

This gets worse if a key is pressed on the keyboard as extra code inside the $EA31 ROM routine is then called to handle the keypress. This is a problem as that frame time could be better used for game code.

- Press **F6** to assemble and run in the VICE emulator.

To view the IRQ interrupt vector in the C64 Debugger:

- Click to the left of the **gameMainIRQ1** label to add a breakpoint.

```
● 52    .break
  53    gameMainIRQ1:
  54        LIBRASTERIRQ_START_V(IrqFast)          // Start the irq
```

- Press **Shift-F6** to assemble and run in the C64 Debugger.
- Press **Ctrl-F2** to switch to the disassembler, data dump and memory map view.
- Mouse over and scroll down the memory map (1) to get to the bottom.

The last two memory locations (**$fffe** and **$ffff**) contain **48** and **ff** (2). ($fff0 is the label for the start of the row).

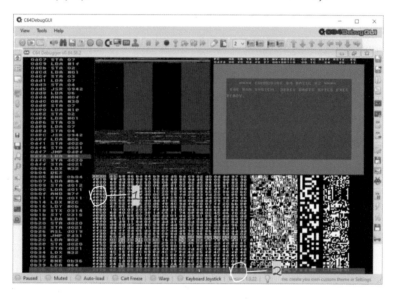

Note that the left hand column shows the same memory locations as the center section, but translated into assembly instructions for easier viewing of code.

Faster IRQ's

Many times when developing a game, the functionality of the $EA31 ROM routine is not required so removing it would free up frame time for other purposes.

A simple way to achieve this is to override the address stored in the IRQ vector ($FFFE-$FFFF) to point straight to our custom IRQ routine.

However, there are 3 caveats:

- The IRQ vector is in Kernal ROM which is read only.
- The $FF48 Kernal ROM routine stores and restores the A, X, and Y registers which is still desirable.
- The $EA31 ROM routine calls an rti instruction to return from the interrupt which is also required.

To get around these issues we can:

- Turn off Kernal ROM to expose RAM instead allowing the IRQ vector to be modified.
- Manually store/restore the A, X and Y registers as part of our custom IRQ routine.
- Call rti when the custom IRQ routine is finished.

Note that as the BASIC ROM uses the Kernal ROM, it must also be turned off. The reverse is not the case. It is possible to turn off the BASIC ROM and leave the Kernal ROM enabled.

Kernal ROM must be turned off for Faster IRQ's to work

Faster IRQ

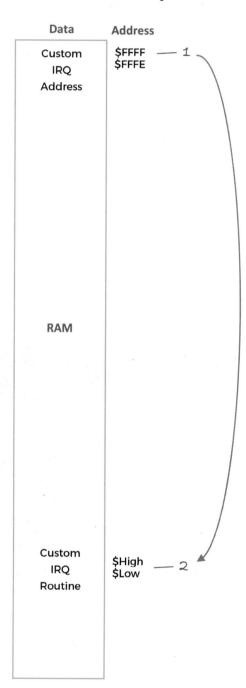

Data

Custom
IRQ
Address

RAM

Custom
IRQ
Routine

Address

$FFFF
$FFFE — 1

$High
$Low — 2

- Switch to the **gameMain2.asm** file.

There are only few small changes required to the code to use faster IRQ's.

The basic and kernal ROM's are disabled with a macro call.

gameMain2.asm

```
gameMainInit:
    // Disable BASIC & Kernal ROMs
    LIBUTILITY_DISABLEBASICANDKERNAL()
    . . .
```

The **IrqFast** constant that is passed into the IRQ macros is changed to **true**. This causes the macros to correctly handle the A, X, & Y registers and also call **rti** (See the Library Code chapter for macro explanations.

gameMain2.asm

```
.const IrqFast = true
    . . .
gameMainIRQ1:
    LIBRASTERIRQ_START_V(IrqFast)          // Start the irq
    LIBSCREEN_SETSCREENCOLOR_V(GREEN)      // Set the screen color
    LIBUTILITY_WAITLOOP_V(50)              // Wait for a while
    // Point to 2nd irq
    LIBRASTERIRQ_SET_VAV(Irq2Scanline, gameMainIRQ2, IrqFast)
    LIBSCREEN_SETSCREENCOLOR_V(WHITE)      // Set the screen color
    LIBRASTERIRQ_END_V(IrqFast)            // End the irq
    . . .
gameMainIRQ2:
    LIBRASTERIRQ_START_V(IrqFast)          // Start the irq
    LIBSCREEN_SETSCREENCOLOR_V(RED)        // Set the screen color
    LIBUTILITY_WAITLOOP_V(50)              // Wait for a while
    LIBRASTERIRQ_SET_VAV(Irq1Scanline, gameMainIRQ1, IrqFast)
    // Point to 1st irq
    LIBSCREEN_SETSCREENCOLOR_V(WHITE)      // Set the screen color
    LIBRASTERIRQ_END_V(IrqFast)            // End the irq
```

The time taken between exiting the custom IRQ routine and returning to the game update code (white bar) is now greatly reduced, and keypresses on the keyboard have no effect.

The contents of the IRQ interrupt vector $FFFE-$FFFF has changed to 026 ($1A) and 011 ($0B) so the memory address of the custom IRQ routine is $0B1A.

- Press **F6** to assemble and run in the VICE emulator.

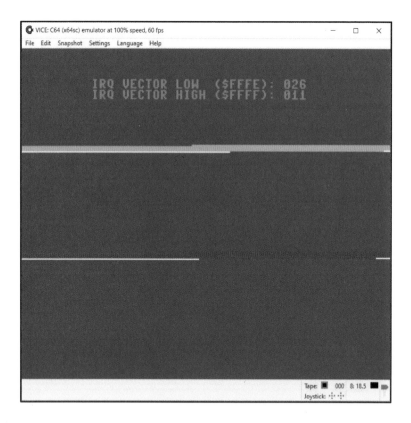

- Click to the left of the **gameMainIRQ1** label to add a breakpoint.

```
● 53    .break
  54   gameMainIRQ1:
  55      LIBRASTERIRQ_START_V(IrqFast)              // Start the irq
```

- Press **Shift-F6** to assemble and run in the C64 Debugger.
- Press **Ctrl-Shift-F3** to switch to the source code view.

The break point memory address for the gameMainIRQ1 custom IRQ routine is $0b1a (1) which is correct.

The source code shows the first instruction which is inside the LIBRASTERIRQ_START_V macro (Click on the address and press up/down arrows to go see the source code before and after).

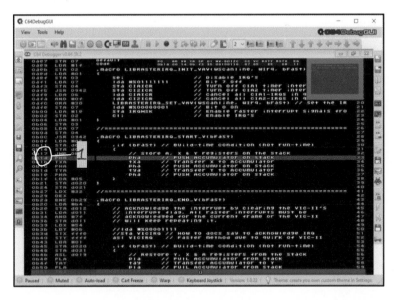

Sprite Multiplexing

The Commodore 64 only has 8 hardware sprites but the actual constraint is 8 sprites per scanline. It's therefore possible to change a sprite's attributes as soon as it has been drawn to allow many more sprites on the screen.

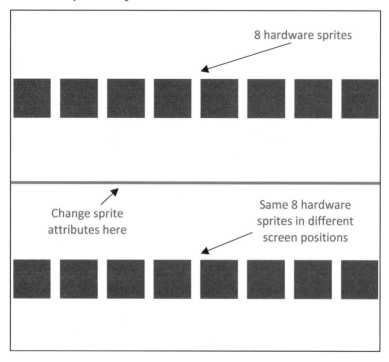

To use sprite multiplexing in the most efficient manner may require a complex algorithm to sort sprites into the correct vertical screen order. However, this depends on the sprite usage required for a particular game.

For the Beach Bar game, sprite multiplexing will be used for the crabs (See Chapter 11) and they are laid out in horizontal formations and are unable to move in the vertical direction. This allows for a much simpler process of drawing sprites, changing attributes, then redrawing sprites and so on..., without any sprite sorting requirements.

- Switch to the **gameMain3.asm** file.

In addition to the fast irq setup from the previous section, the 8 hardware sprites are enabled and the sprite multicolors setup. Then the sprite animations are set for each sprite.

gameMain3.asm

```
gameMainInit:
    . . .
    // Enable all 8 hardware sprites
    LIBSPRITE_ENABLEALL_V(true)
    // Set the sprite multicolor mode
    LIBSPRITE_MULTICOLORENABLEALL_V(true)
    // Set the sprite multicolors
    LIBSPRITE_SETMULTICOLORS_VV(LIGHT_RED, BROWN)
    // Initialize the sprite animations
    GAMEMAIN_SPRITESANIMINIT()
```

To set the animations for each sprite, a loop for SpriteMax (8) times reads the start and end frames from an array before calling the LIBSPRITE_PLAYANIM_AAAVV library macro.

gameMain3.asm

```
.macro GAMEMAIN_SPRITESANIMINIT()
{
    ldx #0  // Start at index 0
    stx bSprite
loop:
    // Read this element's variables
    lda bStartFrameArray,x
    sta bStartFrame
    lda bEndFrameArray,x
    sta bEndFrame
    // Set the sprite animation details
    LIBSPRITE_PLAYANIM_AAAVV(bSprite, bStartFrame, bEndFrame,
 AnimDelay, true)
    // Loop for SpriteMax times
    inx
    inc bSprite
    cpx #SpriteMax
    bne loop
}
```

The player character's sprite data is imported into the program at the $2800 memory location.

gameMain3.asm

```
//==============================================================
// Data

// Add sprite data at the $2800 memory location
*= $2800 "Sprites"
    .import binary "..\..\Content\BeachBarSprites1.bin"
```

This memory location matches with the SPRITERAM label in libDefines.asm (See the **Sprite Pointers** section on **page 133** in the **C64 Programmer's Reference Guide** for more information on sprite memory locations).

libDefines.asm

```
// Sprite Memory
// 160 decimal * 64(sprite size) = 10240(hex $2800)
.label SPRITERAM = 160
```

Sprites have specific memory location requirements

Each custom IRQ routine calls an update macro to change each sprite's positions and colors for a particular row.

gameMain3.asm

```
gameMainIRQ1:
    LIBRASTERIRQ_START_V(IrqFast)    // Start the irq
    GAMEMAIN_SPRITESUPDATE_VV(wXPosRow1Array, Irq1Scanline + S
canlineOffset, BLACK)
    LIBRASTERIRQ_SET_VAV(Irq2Scanline, gameMainIRQ2, IrqFast)
    // Point to 2nd irq
    LIBRASTERIRQ_END_V(IrqFast)      // End the irq
```

The sprite update macro calls the library macros individually rather than in a loop due to the limited frame time available between sprite rows.

gameMain3.asm

```
.macro GAMEMAIN_SPRITESUPDATE_VV(wXPosArray, bYPos, bColor)
{
    // These are unrolled for speed - i.e. not put into a loop
    LIBSCREEN_PROFILESTART()
    LIBSPRITE_SETALLCOLORS_V(bColor)
    LIBSPRITE_SETPOSITION_VAV(0, wXPosArray, bYPos)
    LIBSPRITE_SETPOSITION_VAV(1, wXPosArray + (2*1), bYPos)
    LIBSPRITE_SETPOSITION_VAV(2, wXPosArray + (2*2), bYPos)
    LIBSPRITE_SETPOSITION_VAV(3, wXPosArray + (2*3), bYPos)
    LIBSPRITE_SETPOSITION_VAV(4, wXPosArray + (2*4), bYPos)
    LIBSPRITE_SETPOSITION_VAV(5, wXPosArray + (2*5), bYPos)
    LIBSPRITE_SETPOSITION_VAV(6, wXPosArray + (2*6), bYPos)
    LIBSPRITE_SETPOSITION_VAV(7, wXPosArray + (2*7), bYPos)
    LIBSCREEN_PROFILEEND()
}
```

The position and color changes must be complete before the next row begins to draw or else some of the scanlines of the sprite could draw with the previous sprite row attributes.

Sprite updates must be finished before they are drawn

The LIBSPRITE_UPDATE library macro is called once per frame to update the sprite animation frames.

gameMain3.asm

```
gameMainUpdate:
    LIBSCREEN_WAIT_V(250)    // Wait for scanline 250
    LIBSPRITE_UPDATE()       // Update the sprites
    jmp gameMainUpdate       // Jump back, infinite loop
```

- Press **F6** to assemble and run in the VICE emulator.

The profile bars show the amount of time taken for each custom IRQ routine to update the sprite positions and colors ready for the next sprite row.

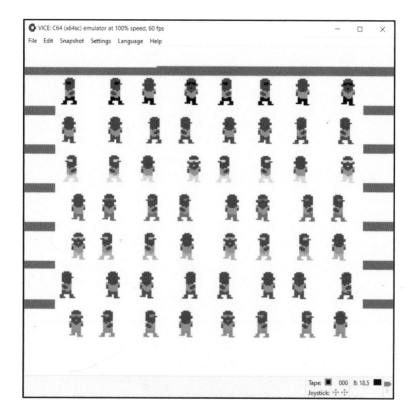

PART II: LET'S MAKE A BEACH BAR GAME

Chapter 5: Wait... What?

It may be useful at this stage to test out the final game we're aiming to develop before we build it from the ground up.

How to Play

- Run **prgs\beachbar.prg** in the VICE emulator or on real Commodore 64/128 hardware.

The game is configured to use a joystick in port 2 (or keys mapped to this joystick in VICE).

The information HUD shows Energy Bar (1), Drink Color Held (2), Drinks Required Yes/No? (3), Towels Required Yes/No? (4), Number of Drinks Available (5), Number of Towels Available (6), Score (7), and High Score (8).

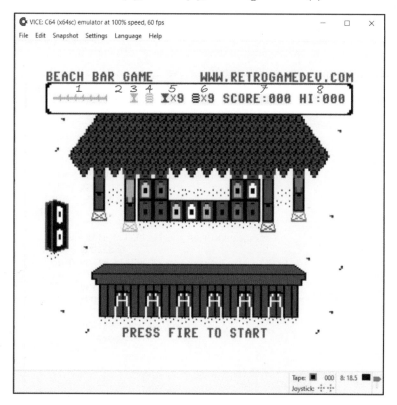

- Press **Fire** to start the game.

The bar customers begin to sit and order drinks. The **Drink Icon** (1) above their head shows the **Drink Color** they require.

- Press **Fire** over a **Drink Crosshatch** (2) to fetch the appropriate **Drink Color**.
- Press **Fire** when over the **Drink Icon** (1) to deliver the drink to the customer.

Taking too long to deliver a drink will cause the customer to leave and the **Energy Bar** to be depleted.

Top Left Screen

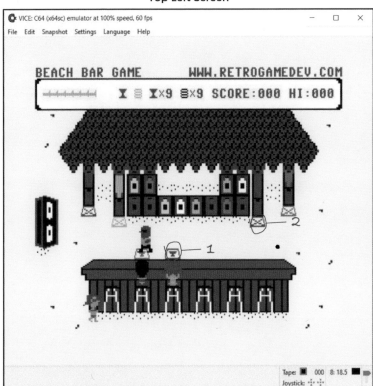

- Press **Fire** over the **Replenish Drinks Icon** (*1*) to replenish the **Number of Drinks Available.**

Touching the crabs will cause the **Energy Bar** to be depleted.

Top Right Screen

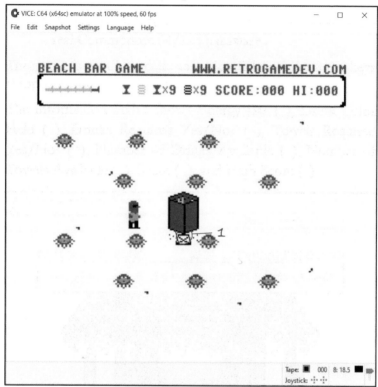

Touching crabs hurts!

The sun lounger customers begin to request towels. They wait next to the sun lounger they have chosen.

- Press **Fire** over a **Sun Lounger Crosshatch** (1) to deliver a towel to the customer.

Taking too long to deliver a towel will cause the customer to leave and the **Energy Bar** to be depleted.

Bottom Left Screen

- Press **Fire** over the **New Towels Icon** (1) to replenish the **Number of Towels Available.**

Touching the crabs will cause the **Energy Bar** to be depleted.

Bottom Right Screen

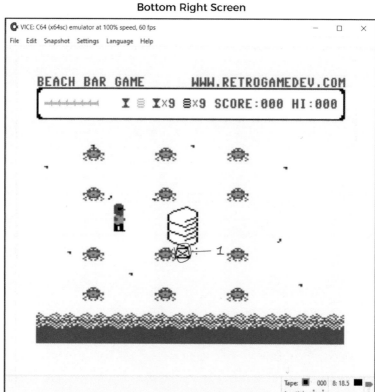

Try to improve your high score.

Chapter 6: Billy the Barman

SpritePad

- Open **BeachBarSprites1.spd** in **SpritePad**.

Included are 8 multicolor frames of character animation.

To preview animation frame sequences:

- Click **multiple frames** + the **Shift** key (1).
- Click the **Send range to Animator** icon (2).
- Click the **Play** icon (3).
- Change the animation speed with the **Timer** value (4).

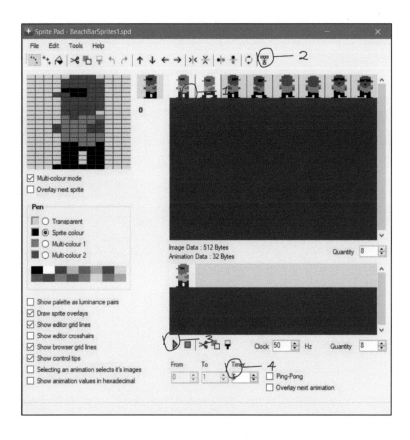

Try creating your own player animations.

To save the sprite data:

- Choose **File->Save Project As...** to save the .spd project file.
- Choose **File->Import/Export...->Raw / PRG->Export Sprite Data...** to export the Raw Data **.bin** file.

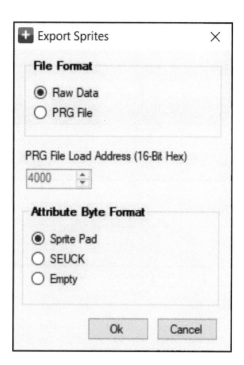

Player Sprite

- Open **Ch6.code-workspace** in **Visual Studio Code**.
- Start with the **gameMain1.asm** file.

In the initialize code, the 8 hardware sprites are enabled and the multicolors are setup (these are global colors for all 8 sprites). Then a subroutine is called to initialize the player.

gameMain1.asm

```
// Enable all 8 hardware sprites
LIBSPRITE_ENABLEALL_V(true)
// Set the sprite multicolor mode
LIBSPRITE_MULTICOLORENABLEALL_V(true)
// Set the sprite multicolors
LIBSPRITE_SETMULTICOLORS_VV(LIGHT_RED, BROWN)

// Call the player initialize subroutine
jsr gamePlayerInit
```

The player sprite is initialized by setting the current animation frame, start position, and color.

Note that sprite X positions use a word rather than a byte because the visible X position on screen can be > 255.

gamePlayer.asm

```
gamePlayerInit:
    // Set sprite animation frame, position, and color
    LIBSPRITE_SETFRAME_AV(bPlayerSprite, PlayerStartFrame)
    LIBSPRITE_SETPOSITION_AAA(bPlayerSprite, wPlayerX, bPlayerY)
    LIBSPRITE_SETCOLOR_AV(bPlayerSprite, BLACK)
    rts
```

The exported sprite data is added to the program by importing it at the correct memory location. The ***= $2800** directive tells the assembler to start placing data at memory location $2800 onwards.

gameMain1.asm

```
// Add sprite data at the $2800 memory location
*= $2800 "Sprites"
    .import binary "..\..\Content\BeachBarSprites1.bin"
```

Sprite colors are set in code, not exported from SpritePad

- Press **F6** to assemble and run in the VICE emulator.

The player sprite is in the starting position using a downward facing animation frame.

Movement and Animation

- Switch to the **gameMain2.asm** file.

A macro and a subroutine call are added to update the player's movement and animation.

The LIBSPRITE_UPDATE library macro handles the actual updating of sprite animation frames at the correct time, allowing the game code to use abstract animation play macros.

gameMain2.asm

```
LIBSPRITE_UPDATE()      // Update the sprites
jsr gamePlayerUpdate    // Update the player subroutines
```

The player's position and animation frame are then updated and the x and y positions are drawn to the screen for debugging purposes.

gamePlayer.asm

```
gamePlayerUpdate:
    jsr gamePlayerUpdatePosition
    jsr gameplayerUpdateAnimation
    // Debug print the position
    LIBSCREEN_DEBUG16BIT_VVA(0, 1, wPlayerX)
    LIBSCREEN_DEBUG8BIT_VVA(2, 2, bPlayerY)
    rts
```

Updating the position consists of checking for a joystick direction press and adding or subtracting the player speed in that direction.

gamePlayer.asm

```
gamePlayerUpdatePosition:
    LIBINPUT_GET_V(GameportLeftMask) // Check left
    bne gPUPRight // If left not pressed, skip to right check
    // Subtract X speed
    LIBMATH_SUB16BIT_AVA(wPlayerX, PlayerSpeed, wPlayerX)
    jmp gPUPEndmove // Skip all other input checks
    . . .
```

Then the player's x and y positions are clamped to the screen bounds and the player position is set to the player sprite.

gamePlayer.asm

```
gamePlayerUpdatePosition:
    . . .
    // clamp the player x position
    LIBMATH_MIN16BIT_AV(wPlayerX, PlayerXMax)
    LIBMATH_MAX16BIT_AV(wPlayerX, PlayerXMin)

    // clamp the player y position
    LIBMATH_MIN8BIT_AV(bPlayerY, PlayerYMax)
    LIBMATH_MAX8BIT_AV(bPlayerY, PlayerYMin)

    // Set the player's sprite position
    LIBSPRITE_SETPOSITION_AAA(bPlayerSprite, wPlayerX,bPlayerY)
```

The five separate animation states are implemented as a jump table, where the current state is stored in a variable and one of the subroutines in the jump table is chosen based on the current state.

Each animation state can jump to any of the other states.

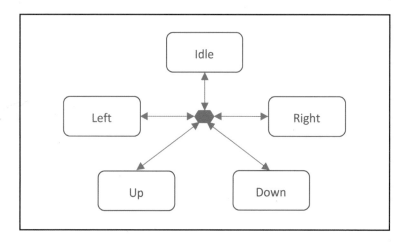

Each subroutine's address is a 16-bit number, therefore they require a word to store.

gamePlayer.asm

```
gamePlayerAnimationJumpTable:
  .word gamePlayerUpdateAnimationIdle
  .word gamePlayerUpdateAnimationLeft
  .word gamePlayerUpdateAnimationRight
  .word gamePlayerUpdateAnimationUp
  .word gamePlayerUpdateAnimationDown
```

Updating the animation consists of using the bPlayerAnim variable as a lookup index into the jump table. The index is multiplied by 2 as each table entry consists of 2 bytes (a word). The low and high bytes are copied into 2 adjacent temporary variables and then an indirect jump is used to the selected subroutine.

gamePlayer.asm

```
gameplayerUpdateAnimation:
  lda bPlayerAnim           // Get the current state into A
  asl                       // X2 as table is in words
  tay                       // Copy A to Y
  lda gamePlayerAnimationJumpTable,y // Lookup low byte
  sta ZeroPage1             // Store in a temporary variable
  lda gamePlayerAnimationJumpTable+1,y // Lookup high byte
  sta ZeroPage2             // Store in temporary variable+1
  jmp (ZeroPage1)           // Indirect jump to subroutine
```

An indirect jump (specified by enclosing the address in brackets) uses the 8-bit address passed in and the 8-bit address+1 to construct a 16-bit memory address to jump to.

With a standard jmp instruction the address is hardcoded, but with an indirect jmp instruction the address can be changed while the program is running.

The state update subroutines check for joystick input and call the appropriate state set subroutine.

gamePlayer.asm

```
gamePlayerUpdateAnimationIdle:
    LIBINPUT_GET_V(GameportLeftMask) // Check left
    bne gPUIRight // If left not pressed, skip to right check
    jsr gamePlayerSetAnimationLeft
gPUIRight:
    LIBINPUT_GET_V(GameportRightMask) // Check right
    bne gPUIUp // If right not pressed, skip to up check
    jsr gamePlayerSetAnimationRight
gPUIUp:
    LIBINPUT_GET_V(GameportUpMask) // Check up
    bne gPUIDown // If up not pressed, skip to down check
    jsr gamePlayerSetAnimationUp
gPUIDown:
    LIBINPUT_GET_V(GameportDownMask) // Check down
    bne gPUIEnd // If down not pressed, skip to end
    jsr gamePlayerSetAnimationDown
gPUIEnd:
    rts
```

The state set subroutines update the player animation state variable, stop the current animation, and start the new animation (if required).

gamePlayer.asm

```
gamePlayerSetAnimationLeft:
    lda #PlayerAnimLeft // Load the state number
    sta bPlayerAnim     // Store the state number
    LIBSPRITE_STOPANIM_A(bPlayerSprite) // Stop existing anims
    // Play the new anim
    LIBSPRITE_PLAYANIM_AVVVV(bPlayerSprite, 0, 1, PlayerAnimDe
lay, true)
    rts
```

- Press **F6** to assemble and run in the VICE emulator.

The player sprite can now walk around using the correct animations and is bound by the screen limits.

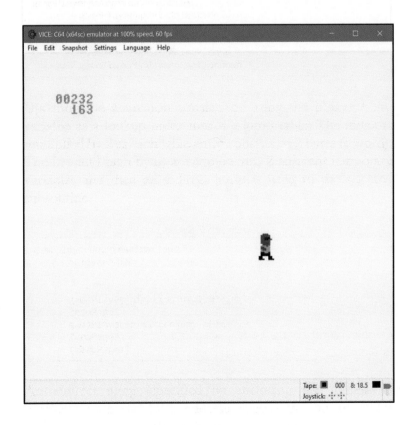

Try changing some of the player Constant values

Chapter 7: Jamaica Mon

CharPad

- Open **BeachBarScreens.ctm** in **CharPad**.

Included is a custom 256 entry character set and a 40x25 screen using those characters.

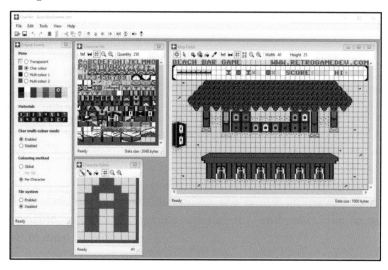

To save memory space the character colors are saved as 1 entry per character in the character set (256 entries) rather than 1 entry per screen location (which would be 1000 entries).

This means that if the same character is required with different colors, the character must be duplicated in the character set.

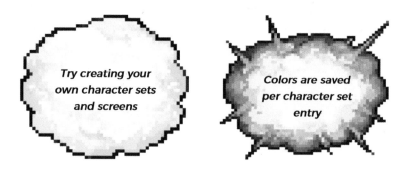

Try creating your own character sets and screens

Colors are saved per character set entry

To save the environment data:

- Choose **File->Save Project As...** to save the .ctm project file.
- Choose **File-> Import/Export->Binary...->Export Character Set...** to save the .bin character set file.
- Choose **File-> Import/Export->Binary...->Export Character Set Attributes...** to save the .bin character set colors file.
- Choose **File-> Import/Export->Binary...->Export Map...** to save the .bin screen file.

There's 1 CharPad project file (**BeachBarScreens.ctm**) and 1 custom character set (**BeachBarScreensCharset.bin**) for all 4 background screens.

- **BeachBarScreenTopLeft.bin**
- **BeachBarScreenTopRight.bin**
- **BeachBarScreenBottomLeft.bin**
- **BeachBarScreenBottomRight.bin**

Swapping the screen files for editing is achieved by importing a different .bin screen file into the same project:

- Choose **File-> Import/Export->Binary...->Import Map...** to import a .bin screen file.

A single character set is shared between all 4 game screens

Display a Background

- Open **Ch7.code-workspace** in **Visual Studio Code**.

The character data is imported at the address to match one of the preset memory slots in libDefines.asm, and passed into the library macro LIBSCREEN_SETCHARMEMORY_V (See the **Character Memory** section on **page 103** in the **C64 Programmer's Reference Guide** for more information on character set memory locations).

The screen data can be placed at any available RAM area.

gameData.asm

```
*= $2000 "Characters" // Add at $2000 memory location
  .import binary "..\..\Content\BeachBarScreensCharset.bin"

//===========================================================
. . .

*= $3080 "Screens" // Add at $3080 memory location
gameDataBackground:
 .import binary "..\..\Content\BeachBarScreenTopLeft.bin"
 .import binary "..\..\Content\BeachBarScreenTopRight.bin"
 .import binary "..\..\Content\BeachBarScreenBottomLeft.bin"
 .import binary "..\..\Content\BeachBarScreenBottomRight.bin"
gameDataBackGroundCol:
 .import binary "..\..\Content\BeachBarScreensColors.bin"
```

In the initialize code, the screen is put into multicolor mode and the screen multicolors are setup. Then the custom character set memory is pointed to, and the screen characters and colors are copied into screen RAM.

gameMain.asm

```
    // Set the background multicolor mode
    LIBSCREEN_SETMULTICOLORMODE_V(true)
    // Set the background multicolors
    LIBSCREEN_SETMULTICOLORS_VV(BLACK, BROWN)
    // Set the custom character set
    LIBSCREEN_SETCHARMEMORY_V(CharacterSlot2000)
    // Set the background screen
    LIBSCREEN_SETBACKGROUND_AA(gameDataBackground + (PlayerSc
reenTopLeft*1000), gameDataBackGroundCol)
```

Screen Switching

A subroutine call is added to the player update to change the screen map when switching screens.

gamePlayer.asm

```
gamePlayerUpdate:
    . . .
    jsr gamePlayerUpdateMap
    rts
```

As with the player animations, a jump table is used to select between different subroutines to call based on the current map screen number. A 16-bit word containing the memory address of each subroutine is stored in the jump table.

gamePlayer.asm

```
gamePlayerMapJumpTable:
    .word gamePlayerUpdateMapTopLeft
    .word gamePlayerUpdateMapTopRight
    .word gamePlayerUpdateMapBottomLeft
    .word gamePlayerUpdateMapBottomRight
```

The update map subroutine works the same as the animation update subroutine but uses the map jump table instead.

gamePlayer.asm

```
gameplayerUpdateMap:
    lda bMapScreen            // Get the current state into A
    asl                       // Multiply by 2
    tay                       // Copy A to Y
    lda gamePlayerMapJumpTable,y // Lookup low byte
    sta ZeroPage1             // Store in a temporary variable
    lda gamePlayerMapJumpTable+1,y // Lookup high byte
    sta ZeroPage2             // Store in temporary variable+1
    jmp (ZeroPage1)           // Indirect jump to subroutine
```

Each screen state can jump to two of the other states.

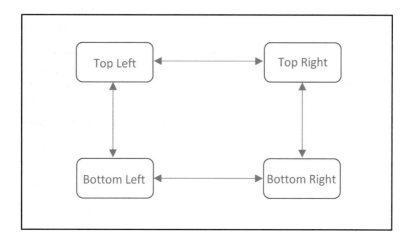

There is one UpdateMap subroutine for each screen that the player can be on.

For example if the player is on the top left screen (the bar screen), then the gamePlayerUpdateMapTopLeft is running which does ...

X Processing:

- If the player X position < player X Max position then skip to Y processing, otherwise ...
- Set player X position to player X Min position and ...
- Set screen to top right

Y Processing:

- If the player Y position < player Y Max position then skip to end, otherwise ...
- Set player Y position to player Y Min position and ...
- Set screen to bottom left

The other 3 subroutines work in a similar manner but switch
to screens in different directions.

gamePlayer.asm

```
gamePlayerUpdateMapTopLeft:
    // X direction
    lda wPlayerX+1 // If high byte is 0 skip X processing
    beq gPUS1EndX

    lda wPlayerX // If low byte < PlayerXMax skip X processing
    cmp #<PlayerXMax
    bmi gPUS1EndX

    lda #>PlayerXMin // Set player X position to XMin
    sta wPlayerX+1
    lda #PlayerXMin+1
    sta wPlayerX

    // Set screen to top right
    LIBSCREEN_SETBACKGROUND_AA(gameDataBackground + (PlayerSc
reenTopRight*1000), gameDataBackGroundCol)
    lda #PlayerScreenTopRight
    sta bMapScreen

gPUS1EndX:
    // Y direction
    lda bPlayerY //If PlayerY < PlayerYMax skip Y processsing
    cmp #PlayerYMax
    bmi gPUS1EndY

    lda #PlayerYMin+1 // Set player Y position to YMin
    sta bPlayerY

    // Set screen to bottom left
    LIBSCREEN_SETBACKGROUND_AA(gameDataBackground + (PlayerSc
reenBottomLeft*1000), gameDataBackGroundCol)
    lda #PlayerScreenBottomLeft
    sta bMapScreen

gPUS1EndY:
    rts
```

- Press **F6** to assemble and run in the VICE emulator.

The background screen displays along with the player sprite.

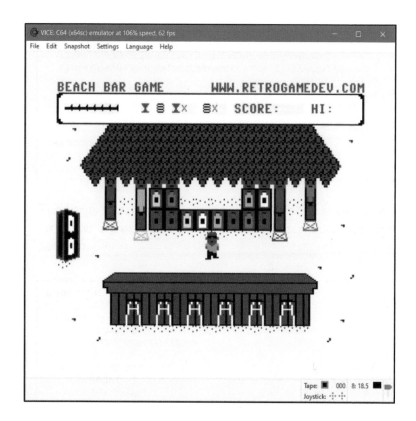

Try walking around the 4 screens

Chapter 8: Things That Go Bump

- Open **Ch8.code-workspace** in **Visual Studio Code**.

Collision Points

A subroutine call is added to the player update to perform background collisions. This stops the player from passing through some of the background graphics.

gamePlayer.asm

```
gamePlayerUpdate:
    . . .
    jsr gamePlayerUpdateBackgroundCollisions
    . . .
    rts
```

Points are defined for the left, right, and bottom. They are relative to the top left (0,0) of the sprite.

gamePlayer.asm

```
.const PlayerLeftPointX     = 5
.const PlayerRightPointX    = 20
.const PlayerPointY         = 31 // 50-19
```

From these 3 points a bottom left collision (1) and a bottom right collision (2) are performed.

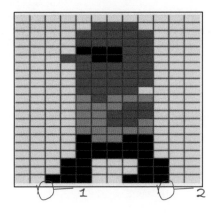

There's also a 50 pixel offset adjustment for the Y point because that's the Y position the sprite needs to be to make it fully visible at the top of the screen and aligned with the first row of screen characters.

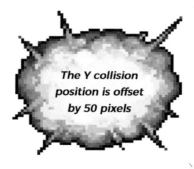

The Y collision position is offset by 50 pixels

Collision Detection and Response

The gamePlayerUpdateBackgroundCollisions subroutine transforms the player's current position by the left collision points then calls the gamePlayerUpdateCollisionsCollide subroutine to perform the collision response. The same is performed for the right collision points.

After the collisions, the player's new position is stored ready for use the next frame by the collision response subroutine.

gamePlayer.asm

```
gamePlayerUpdateBackgroundCollisions:
    // Left point
    LIBMATH_SUB16BIT_AVA(wPlayerX, PlayerLeftPointX, wPlayerCol
lisionX)
    LIBMATH_SUB8BIT_AVA(bPlayerY, PlayerPointY, bPlayerCollisio
nY)

    jsr gamePlayerUpdateCollisionsCollide

    // Right point
    LIBMATH_SUB16BIT_AVA(wPlayerX, PlayerRightPointX, wPlayerCo
llisionX)

    jsr gamePlayerUpdateCollisionsCollide

    // Store previous player position
    lda wPlayerX+1
    sta wPlayerPreviousX+1
    lda wPlayerX
    sta wPlayerPreviousX
    lda bPlayerY
    sta bPlayerPreviousY
    rts
```

Try adjusting the collision points to see how it affects the player collisions

The gamePlayerUpdateCollisionsCollide subroutine performs 4 distinct stages to determine if a collision point collided with a certain background character, and whether or not to reset the player back to a previous position.

The 4 stages are:

- Find the background character x and y from the pixel x and y.
- Find the background character ID at the character x and y.
- Check if the background character ID > PlayerCharCollIndex.
- If so, it's a collision so reset player to previous position.

gamePlayer.asm

```
gamePlayerUpdateCollisionsCollide:
    // Stage 1 - Find the character x & y from the pixel x & y
    LIBSCREEN_PIXELTOCHAR_AAAA(wPlayerCollisionX, bPlayerCollis
ionY, bPlayerXChar, bPlayerYChar)

    // Stage 2 - Get the character ID from the character x & y
    LIBSCREEN_GETCHARACTER_AAA(bPlayerXChar, bPlayerYChar, Zero
Page1)

    // Stage 3 - Check if character ID > PlayerCharCollIndex
    lda #PlayerCharCollIndex
    cmp ZeroPage1
    bcs gPUCCNoCollision

    // Stage 4 - Collision response reset to previous position
    lda wPlayerPreviousX+1
    sta wPlayerX+1
    lda wPlayerPreviousX
    sta wPlayerX
    lda bPlayerPreviousY
    sta bPlayerY

gPUCCNoCollision:
    rts
```

In CharPad the characters have been created in such a way that character ID's > PlayerCharCollIndex (which has been set to 100) (1) are collidable. The player can walk straight over ID's below that.

Hovering the mouse pointer over a character will display its index.

Try adjusting PlayerCollIndex to make different characters collidable

Finally the code to set the player sprite's position is separated out into its own subroutine so that it can occur after the background collisions have taken place.

gamePlayer.asm

```
gamePlayerUpdate:
    . . .
    jsr gameplayerUpdateSprite
    rts
```

- Press **F6** to assemble and run in the VICE emulator.

The player now collides with the background.

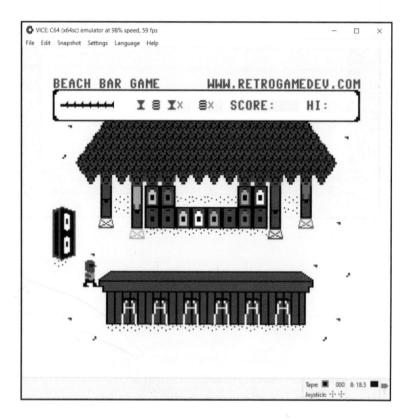

Chapter 9: I Need a Drink

- Open **Ch9.code-workspace** in **Visual Studio Code**.

Variable Arrays

There are a maximum of 6 bar customers at any time (1 for each chair at the bar). The variables used to track the state of each bar customer such as position, state, current chair etc. are stored in variable arrays. There are 6 entries in each variable array (1 for each bar customer).

gameBar.asm

```
// arrays
bBarStateArray:          .byte   0,  0,  0,  0,  0,  0
wBarXArray:              .byte   0,  0,  0,  0,  0,  0
bBarYArray:              .byte   0,  0,  0,  0,  0,  0
bBarWalkDirArray:        .byte   0,  0,  0,  0,  0,  0
bBarTimerHArray:         .byte   0,  0,  0,  0,  0,  0
bBarTimerLArray:         .byte   0,  0,  0,  0,  0,  0
bBarChairTakenArray:     .byte   0,  0,  0,  0,  0,  0
bBarChairArray:          .byte   0,  1,  2,  3,  4,  5
. . .

// current element values
bBarSprite:      .byte 0
bBarState:       .byte 0
bBarElement:     .byte 0
wBarX:           .word 0
bBarY:           .byte 0
bBarWalkDir:     .byte 0
bBarChair:       .byte 0
. . .
```

The update subroutines loop through each bar customer, copy the current bar customer's array values into the current element values, do any updates required, then copy the updated values back to the variable arrays.

Customers

The random numbers are seeded using a built in timer register so that the game plays differently each time. Then subroutine calls are added to initialize and update the bar gameplay.

gameMain.asm

```
// Seed the random number lists
LIBMATH_RANDSEED_AA(bMathRandomCurrent1, TIMALO)
LIBMATH_RANDSEED_AA(bMathRandomCurrent2, TIMALO)
. . .

jsr gameBarInit        // Call the bar initialize subroutine
. . .

gameMainUpdate:
. . .
jsr gameBarUpdate // Update the bar subroutines
```

The bar is initialized by looping through each bar customer to set some defaults including the start timer value and sprite position.

gameBar.asm

```
gameBarInit:
    ldx #0
gBILoop:
    inc bBarSprite // x+1
    jsr gameBarGetVariables
    lda #0
    sta bBarState
    sta wBarX
    sta bBarWalkDir
    // Fill the chair
    lda #True
    sta bBarChairTakenArray,x
    // Get a random timerhigh wait time (0->5)
    LIBMATH_RAND_AAA(bMathRandoms2, bMathRandomCurrent2, wBar
Timer+1)
    // Get a random timerlow wait time (0->255)
    LIBMATH_RAND_AAA(bMathRandoms1, bMathRandomCurrent1, wBarT
imer)
    jsr gameBarSetVariables
    LIBSPRITE_SETPOSITION_AAA(bBarSprite, wBarX, bBarY)
    inx
    cpx #BarSpriteMax
    bne gBILoop
    rts
```

The 16-bit timer value (wBarTimer) is initialized with random values for the high byte (0->5) and low byte (0->255) for the waiting time between states. E.g. how long to wait for a drink to be served, or how long to spend drinking.

The update subroutine loops through each customer, updates the state, then updates the sprites if currently on the bar screen. This is because if not displaying the bar screen the simulation still needs to run but the sprites will be used for the currently displayed screen.

gameBar.asm

```
gameBarUpdate:
    ldx #0
    stx bBarSprite
gBULoop:
    inc bBarSprite // x+1
    jsr gameBarGetVariables
    jsr gameBarUpdateState
    jsr gameBarSetVariables
    // only if on bar screen
    lda bMapScreen
    bne gBUNotOnBarScreen
    jsr gameBarUpdateSprite
gBUNotOnBarScreen:
    inx
    cpx #BarSpriteMax
    bne gBULoop
    rts
```

The 3 gameplay states (Walking, Waiting, and Drinking) are implemented with 2 jump tables (1 for the simulation and 1 for the sprite updates).

gameBar.asm

```
gameBarUpdateStateJumpTable:
    .word gameBarUpdateStateWalking
    .word gameBarUpdateStateWaiting
    .word gameBarUpdateStateDrinking

gameBarUpdateSpriteJumpTable:
    .word gameBarUpdateSpriteWalking
    .word gameBarUpdateSpriteWaiting
    .word gameBarUpdateSpriteDrinking
```

Walking State

The walking state is where the bar customers walk left and right across the screen and is the default on game start.

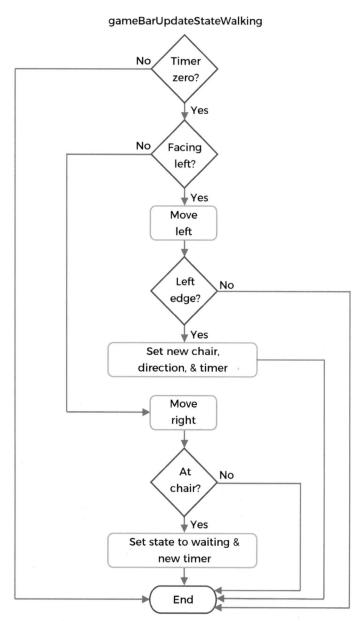

*Try matching the
Walking State
flowchart to the
gameBarUpdateState
Walking code*

The sprite is updated by setting the left or right walking animation and clearing the drink icon (drawn to the screen while in a previous waiting state).

gameBar.asm

```
gameBarUpdateSpriteWalking:

    lda bBarWalkDir
    beq gBUSWRight

// ------------ Walking Left ---------------------

    LIBSPRITE_PLAYANIM_AAAVV(bBarSprite, bBarWalk3, bBarWalk4,
BarAnimDelay, true)
    jmp gBUSpWaEnd

// ------------ Walking Right --------------------

gBUSWRight:

    LIBSPRITE_PLAYANIM_AAAVV(bBarSprite, bBarWalk1, bBarWalk2,
BarAnimDelay, true)

// ------------------------------------------------

gBUSpWaEnd:

    // Clear the drink icon
    LIBSCREEN_SETCHARACTER_S_AAV(bBarDrinkColumn1, bBarDrinkRo
w, Space)
    LIBSCREEN_SETCHARACTER_S_AAV(bBarDrinkColumn2, bBarDrinkRo
w, Space)

    rts
```

Waiting State

The waiting state is where the bar customers sit on the bar stools with a drink icon above their head waiting for a drink.

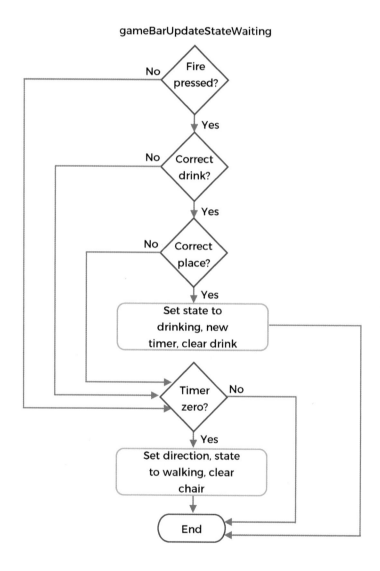

Try matching the Waiting State flowchart to the gameBarUpdateState Waiting code

The sprite is updated by stopping the animation, setting the sitting frame, and drawing the correct drink icon above the bar customer's head.

gameBar.asm

```
gameBarUpdateSpriteWaiting:

    // Draw the sitting sprite
    LIBSPRITE_STOPANIM_A(bBarSprite)
    LIBSPRITE_SETFRAME_AA(bBarSprite, bBarSit)

    // Draw the drink icon
    LIBSCREEN_SETCHARACTER_S_AAA(bBarDrinkColumn1, bBarDrinkRo
w, bBarDrinkChar1)
    LIBSCREEN_SETCOLOR_S_AAA(bBarDrinkColumn1, bBarDrinkRow, b
BarDrinkColor)
    LIBSCREEN_SETCHARACTER_S_AAA(bBarDrinkColumn2, bBarDrinkRo
w, bBarDrinkChar2)
    LIBSCREEN_SETCOLOR_S_AAA(bBarDrinkColumn2, bBarDrinkRow, b
BarDrinkColor)

    rts
```

Drinking State

The drinking state is where the bar customers sit on the bar stools, drinking their drink with no icon above their head.

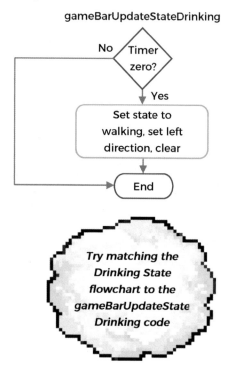

The sprite is updated by stopping the animation, setting the sitting frame, and clearing the drink icon.

gameBar.asm

```
gameBarUpdateSpriteDrinking:

    // Draw the sitting sprite
    LIBSPRITE_STOPANIM_A(bBarSprite)
    LIBSPRITE_SETFRAME_AA(bBarSprite, bBarSit)

    // Clear the drink icon
    LIBSCREEN_SETCHARACTER_S_AAV(bBarDrinkColumn1, bBarDrinkRo
w, Space)
    LIBSCREEN_SETCHARACTER_S_AAV(bBarDrinkColumn2, bBarDrinkRo
w, Space)

    rts
```

- Press **F6** to assemble and run in the VICE emulator.

The customers now go to the bar and order drinks. If they receive the correct drink they'll drink for a while before leaving. If they're left waiting for too long they'll also leave. Note that sprites are displayed incorrectly on other screens until those screens are implemented.

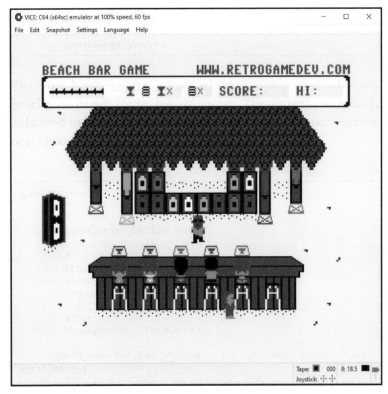

Try serving up some drinks

Chapter 10: Sun Worship

Open **Ch10.code-workspace** in **Visual Studio Code**.

Variable Arrays

There are a maximum of 6 beachgoers at any time (1 for each sun lounger). The variables work the same way as the bar in that there is 1 array entry for each beachgoer and these are fed though the current element variables.

gameLoungers.asm

```
// arrays
bLoungersStateArray:        .byte  0,  0,  0,  0,  0,  0
bLoungersXArray:            .byte  0,  0,  0,  0,  0,  0
bLoungersYArray:            .byte  0,  0,  0,  0,  0,  0
bLoungersWalkDirArray:      .byte  0,  0,  0,  0,  0,  0
bLoungersTimerHArray:       .byte  0,  0,  0,  0,  0,  0
bLoungersTimerLArray:       .byte  0,  0,  0,  0,  0,  0
bLoungersChairTakenArray:   .byte  0,  0,  0,  0,  0,  0
bLoungersChairArray:        .byte  0,  1,  2,  3,  4,  5
. . .
// current element values
bLoungersSprite:      .byte 0
bLoungersState:       .byte 0
bLoungersElement:     .byte 0
wLoungersX:           .word 0
bLoungersY:           .byte 0
bLoungersWalkDir:     .byte 0
bLoungersChair:       .byte 0
. . .
```

Try changing some of the array variable values to see the effects

Beachgoers

The subroutine calls are added to initialize and update the sun lounger gameplay.

gameMain.asm

```
    // Call the loungers initialize subroutine
    jsr gameLoungersInit
    . . .

gameMainUpdate:
    . . .
    jsr gameLoungersUpdate // Update the loungers subroutines
```

The sun loungers are initialized by looping through each beachgoer to set some default values. The timer is purposely defaulted to be higher than the bar customers in order that the beachgoers appear later when the game is started.

gameLoungers.asm

```
gameLoungersInit:
    ldx #0
gLILoop:
    jsr gameLoungersGetVariables
    // Reset some variables
    lda #0
    sta bLoungersState
    sta wLoungersX
    sta bLoungersWalkDir
    // Fill the chair
    lda #True
    sta bLoungersChairTakenArray,x
    // Get a random timerhigh wait time (0->5)
    LIBMATH_RAND_AAA(bMathRandoms2, bMathRandomCurrent2, wLoun
gersTimer+1)
    // Add a large minimum delay to start a little later than
the bar game
    LIBMATH_ADD8BIT_AVA(wLoungersTimer+1, 7, wLoungersTimer+1)
    // Get a random timerlow wait time (0->255)
    LIBMATH_RAND_AAA(bMathRandoms1, bMathRandomCurrent1, wLoun
gersTimer)
    jsr gameLoungersSetVariables
    inx
    cpx #LoungersSpriteMax
    bne gLILoop
    rts
```

The update subroutine loops through each beachgoer, updates the state, then updates the sprites if currently on the sun lounger screen. This is similar the bar update in that the simulation always runs, with the difference being the screen that it will update the sprites on.

```
gameLoungersUpdate:
    ldx #0
    stx bLoungersSprite
gLULoop:
    inc bLoungersSprite // x+1
    jsr gameLoungersGetVariables
    jsr gameLoungersUpdateState
    jsr gameLoungersSetVariables
    // only if on loungers screen
    lda bMapScreen
    cmp #2
    bne gLUNotOnLoungersScreen
    jsr gameLoungersUpdateSprite
gLUNotOnLoungersScreen:
    inx
    cpx #LoungersSpriteMax
    bne gLULoop
    rts
```

The 3 gameplay states (Walking, Waiting, And Lying) are implemented with 2 jump tables (1 for the simulation and 1 for the sprite updates).

gameLoungers.asm

```
gameLoungersUpdateStateJumpTable:
    .word gameLoungersUpdateStateWalking
    .word gameLoungersUpdateStateWaiting
    .word gameLoungersUpdateStateLying

gameLoungersUpdateSpriteJumpTable:
    .word gameLoungersUpdateSpriteWalking
    .word gameLoungersUpdateSpriteWaiting
    .word gameLoungersUpdateSpriteLying
```

84

Walking State

The walking state is the same as for the bar except that the bLoungersWalkYArray has different Y values for the loungers.

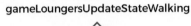

gameLoungersUpdateStateWalking

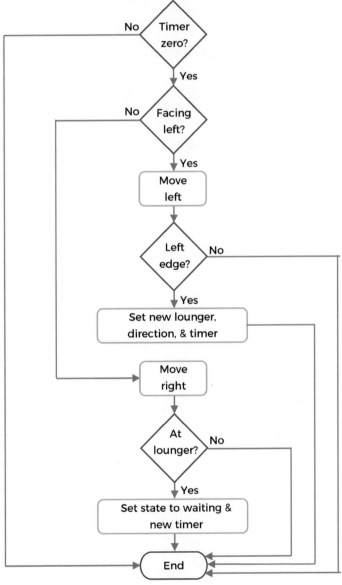

Try matching the Walking State flowchart to the gameLoungersUpdateState Walking code

The sprite is updated by setting the left or right walking animation and drawing the current lounger without a towel.

gameLoungers.asm

```
gameLoungersUpdateSpriteWalking:
    lda bLoungersWalkDir
    beq gLUSpWaRight

// ------------ Walking Left ---------------------

    LIBSPRITE_PLAYANIM_AAAVV(bLoungersSprite, bLoungersWalk3,
bLoungersWalk4, LoungersAnimDelay, true)
    jmp gLUSpWaEnd

// ------------ Walking Right -------------------

gLUSpWaRight:
    LIBSPRITE_PLAYANIM_AAAVV(bLoungersSprite, bLoungersWalk1,
bLoungersWalk2, LoungersAnimDelay, true)

// ------------------------------------------------

gLUSpWaEnd:
    // Draw the lounger without a towel
    LIBSCREEN_SETCHARACTER_S_AAV(bLoungersChairColumn1, bLoung
ersChairRow1, LoungersNoTowel_1_1)
    LIBSCREEN_SETCHARACTER_S_AAV(bLoungersChairColumn2, bLoung
ersChairRow1, LoungersNoTowel_2_1)
    LIBSCREEN_SETCHARACTER_S_AAV(bLoungersChairColumn1, bLoung
ersChairRow2, LoungersNoTowel_1_2)
    LIBSCREEN_SETCHARACTER_S_AAV(bLoungersChairColumn2, bLoung
ersChairRow2, LoungersNoTowel_2_2)
    LIBSCREEN_SETCHARACTER_S_AAV(bLoungersChairColumn1, bLoung
ersChairRow3, LoungersNoTowel_1_3)
    LIBSCREEN_SETCHARACTER_S_AAV(bLoungersChairColumn2, bLoung
ersChairRow3, LoungersNoTowel_2_3)
    rts
```

Waiting State

The waiting state is where the beachgoers stand in front of the sun loungers waiting for a towel to be laid down.

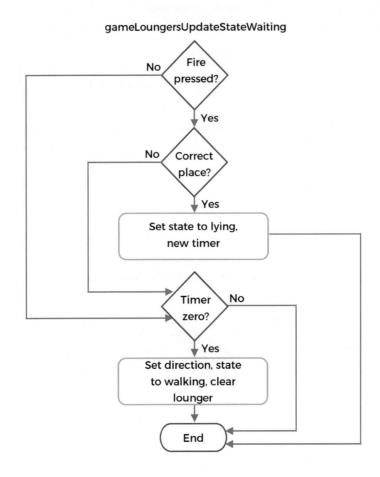

Try matching the Waiting State flowchart to the gameLoungersUpdateState Waiting code

The sprite is updated by stopping the animation, and setting the standing frame.

gameLoungers.asm

```
gameLoungersUpdateSpriteWaiting:
    // Draw the standing sprite
    LIBSPRITE_STOPANIM_A(bLoungersSprite)
    LIBSPRITE_SETFRAME_AA(bLoungersSprite, bLoungersWalk1)
    rts
```

Lying State

The lying state is where the beachgoers lie on the sun loungers with a towel underneath them.

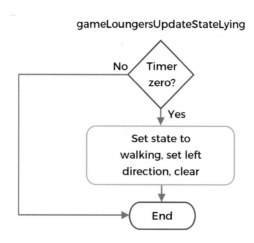

gameLoungersUpdateStateLying

Try matching the Lying State flowchart to the gameLoungersUpdateState Lying code

The sprite is updated by stopping the animation, setting the lying frame, and drawing the current lounger with a towel.

gameLoungers.asm

```
gameLoungersUpdateSpriteLying:
    // Draw the lying sprite
    LIBSPRITE_STOPANIM_A(bLoungersSprite)
    LIBSPRITE_SETFRAME_AA(bLoungersSprite, bLoungersLie)

    // Draw the lounger with a towel
    LIBSCREEN_SETCHARACTER_S_AAV(bLoungersChairColumn1, bLoung
ersChairRow1, LoungersTowel_1_1)
    LIBSCREEN_SETCHARACTER_S_AAV(bLoungersChairColumn2, bLoung
ersChairRow1, LoungersTowel_2_1)
    LIBSCREEN_SETCHARACTER_S_AAV(bLoungersChairColumn1, bLoung
ersChairRow2, LoungersTowel_1_2)
    LIBSCREEN_SETCHARACTER_S_AAV(bLoungersChairColumn2, bLoung
ersChairRow2, LoungersTowel_2_2)
    LIBSCREEN_SETCHARACTER_S_AAV(bLoungersChairColumn1, bLoung
ersChairRow3, LoungersTowel_1_3)
    LIBSCREEN_SETCHARACTER_S_AAV(bLoungersChairColumn2, bLoung
ersChairRow3, LoungersTowel_2_3)
    rts
```

- Press **F6** to assemble and run in the VICE emulator.

The beachgoers now wait in front of the sun loungers. If they receive a towel they'll lie for a while before leaving. If they're left waiting for too long they'll also leave. Note that sprites are displayed incorrectly on other screens until those screens are implemented.

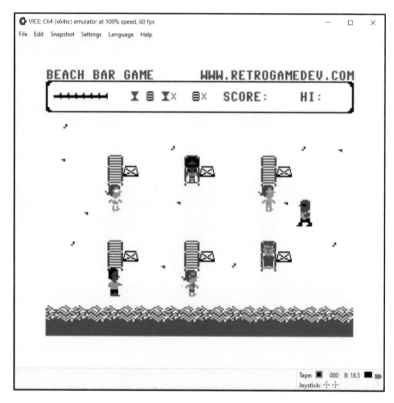

Try delivering some towels

Chapter 11: A Bit Nippy

- Open **Ch11.code-workspace** in **Visual Studio Code**.

Interrupts

The crabs use the interrupt library macros (see Chapter 4) to do sprite multiplexing in order to display 12 crab sprites.

The LIBRASTERIRQ_INIT_VAV macro is called first to start raster IRQ's happening every frame.

The gameCrabsUpdate subroutine is called in the main game loop to update the crab's x movements.

Then the 2 custom interrupt routines are triggered at scanlines 10 and 140 to call separate crab update subroutines (Top and Bottom) which set the top 6 and bottom 6 crab positions.

gameMain.asm

```
    // Constants
    .const IrqFast = true
    .const Irq1Scanline = 10
    .const Irq2Scanline = 140
//============================================================
    . . .
    // Initialize the irq
    LIBRASTERIRQ_INIT_VAV(Irq1Scanline, gameMainIRQ1, IrqFast)
//============================================================
    . . .
    jsr gameCrabsUpdate       // Update the crabs subroutines
    . . .
//============================================================
// Interrupt Handlers
gameMainIRQ1:
    LIBRASTERIRQ_START_V(IrqFast)     // Start the irq
    jsr gameCrabsUpdateTop
    // Point to the 2nd irq
    LIBRASTERIRQ_SET_VAV(Irq2Scanline, gameMainIRQ2, IrqFast)
    LIBRASTERIRQ_END_V(IrqFast)       // End the irq
//============================================================
gameMainIRQ2:
    LIBRASTERIRQ_START_V(IrqFast)     // Start the irq
    jsr gameCrabsUpdateBottom
    // Point to the 1st irq
    LIBRASTERIRQ_SET_VAV(Irq1Scanline, gameMainIRQ1, IrqFast)
    LIBRASTERIRQ_END_V(IrqFast)       // End the irq
```

Movement

The gameCrabsUpdate subroutine loops through sprites 1-6 (0 is for the player) and sets the animation frames and color.

Then the gameCrabsUpdateXOffset subroutine is called that slides the bCrabsXOffset value back and forth between 0 and CrabsOffsetXMax (70).

gameCrabs.asm

```
gameCrabsUpdateXOffset:
    // Skip every other frame to slow down crabs movement
    lda bCrabsSkipMove
    eor #1          // Toggle
    sta bCrabsSkipMove
    bne gCUXEnd
    lda bCrabsXOffsetLeft
    beq gCUXRight   // If moving right jump to gCUXRight

    // Left directional movement
gCUXLeft:
    dec bCrabsXOffset// Move left by 1
    bne gCUXEnd     // If not at 0, jmp to end
    lda #False      // If at 0, toggle left flag
    sta bCrabsXOffsetLeft
    jmp gCUXEnd     // Skip over right movement

    // Right directional movement
gCUXRight:
    inc bCrabsXOffset // Move right by 1
    lda bCrabsXOffset
    cmp #CrabsOffsetXMax
    bne gCUXEnd     // If not at CrabsOffsetXMax, jmp to end
    lda #True       // If at CrabsOffsetXMax, toggle left flag
    sta bCrabsXOffsetLeft
gCUXEnd:
    rts
```

Try changing the CrabsOffsetXMax value

X > 255 will wrap around as bytes are being used for x arrays

The gameCrabsUpdateTop subroutine (called from the raster interrupt) loops through sprites 1-6 and applies the x offset to the sprite position.

gameCrabs.asm

```
. . .
bCrabsDirArray:        .byte   0,  0,  0,  1,  1,  1
. . .
    // Apply x offset to position
    lda bCrabsDir
    beq gCUTNotReverseDir
    // Add if going right
    LIBMATH_SUB8BIT_AAA(wCrabsX, bCrabsXOffset, wCrabsX)
    jmp gCUTReverseDirEnd
gCUTNotReverseDir:
    // Subtract if going left
    LIBMATH_ADD8BIT_AAA(wCrabsX, bCrabsXOffset, wCrabsX)
gCUTReverseDirEnd:

    // Set the sprite position
    LIBSPRITE_SETPOSITION_AAA(bCrabsSprite, wCrabsX, bCrabsY)
    . . .
```

This is based on the bCrabsDirArray entry to say whether it should be the left or right direction, so 3 sprites have the offset subtracted and 3 sprites have it added.

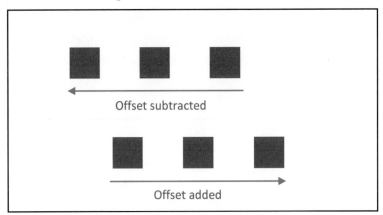

The gameCrabsUpdateBottom subroutine doesn't need to recalculate the x positions as it uses the same values. The only thing that changes is the y positions.

Collisions

Detecting collisions between the player and the crabs uses the VIC-II built in pixel collision functionality. This tells us that a collision has occurred but not the exact sprite the player has collided with (this is ok as all crab collisions are handled the same way).

A call to the gameplayerUpdateSpriteCollisions subroutine is added to gamePlayerUpdate.

gamePlayer.asm

```
gamePlayerUpdate:
    . . .
    jsr gamePlayerUpdateSpriteCollisions
    . . .
    rts
```

If a collision is detected then the player sprite color is set to red. A frame wait is implemented so that energy isn't decreased every frame.

gamePlayer.asm

```
gamePlayerUpdateSpriteCollisions:
    LIBSPRITE_SETCOLOR_AV(bPlayerSprite, BLACK)

    // Only do if on Top Right or Bottom Right screen
    lda bPlayerMapScreen
    cmp #PlayerScreenTopRight
    beq gPUSCOK
    cmp #PlayerScreenBottomRight
    beq gPUSCOK
    jmp gPUSCEnd
gPUSCOK:
    // If sprite collided, set player sprite color to RED
    LIBSPRITE_DIDCOLLIDESP_A(bPlayerSprite)
    beq gPUSCEnd
    LIBSPRITE_SETCOLOR_AV(bPlayerSprite, RED)
    // Only decrease energy after PlayerSpriteCollWait
    dec bPlayerSpriteCollision
    bne gPUSCEnd
    // Will decrease energy here
    lda #PlayerSpriteCollWait
    sta bPlayerSpriteCollision
gPUSCEnd:
    rts
```

- Press **F6** to assemble and run in the VICE emulator.

The crabs now move side to side on the Top Right and Bottom Right screens. If the player collides with a crab then the player's sprite color will turn red.

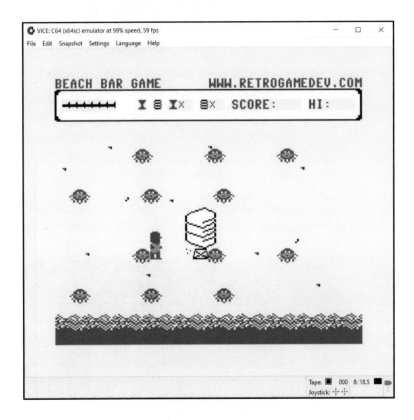

Try getting to the drink or towel refill without turning red

Chapter 12: Let Me Hear Ya

- Open **Ch12.code-workspace** in **Visual Studio Code**.

SID Files

The Commodore 64 uses the SID (Sound Interface Device) chip to play back music and sound effects.

SID files (**.sid** extension) contain both the audio data and the program code used for playback and are created with music tracker software such as GoatTracker 2.

The creation of these files is beyond the scope of this book but there are vast collections of free SID files available from sites such as hvsc.c64.org.

E.g. A search for the word **beach** produces the following:

SID files need to be imported to a specific memory address which can be located in the **Tune Details**, $1000 in this example (1).

The libSound library macros assume the **Init Address** is the same as the **Load Address** and the **Play Address** is the **Init Address + 3**.

Load / Init / Play Address must match game values

SID Player

- Start with the **gameMain1.asm** file.

The sound is initialized by passing the SID file memory address to the LIBSOUND_INIT_A macro.

The SID file is imported at the memory address that matches the required Load Address from the Tune Details. Note the SID file has a 126 byte ($7E) header that must be skipped.

gameMain1.asm

```
. . .
    LIBSOUND_INIT_A(gameMainSID)    // Initialize the sound
. . .
// Add sound data at the $1000 memory location
*= $1000 "Sounds"
gameMainSID:
    // $7E is the size of the header to be skipped
    .import binary "..\..\Content\Bahama_Beach.sid", $7E
```

In a raster interrupt routine the LIBSOUND_UPDATE_A macro is called once per frame to update the sound playing.

gameMain1.asm

```
gameMainIRQ1:
    LIBRASTERIRQ_START_V(IrqFast)      // Start the irq
    LIBSOUND_UPDATE_A(gameMainSID)     // Update the sound player
    LIBRASTERIRQ_END_V(IrqFast)        // End the irq
```

- Press **F6** to assemble and run in the VICE emulator.

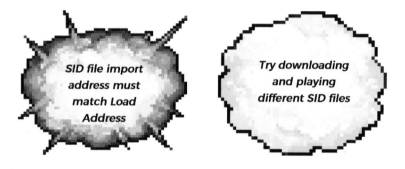

SID file import address must match Load Address

Try downloading and playing different SID files

Game Music and Sfx

- Switch to the **gameMain2.asm** file.

The Beach Bar game music is implemented as the previous section but with the SID file imported in the gameData.asm file along with all the other data.

gameData.asm

```
// Add sound data at the $1000 memory location
*= $1000 "Sound Data"
gameDataSID:
    // $7E is the size of the header to be skipped
    .import binary "..\..\Content\Calypso_Bar.sid", $7E
```

The sound effect data has also been created in GoatTracker 2 and the instrument data exported as a set of byte lists.

gameData.asm

```
SFX_Crab:          .byte $0E,$EE,$00,$DC,$81,$DC,$DC,$DC . . .
SFX_Fail1:         .byte $0E,$EE,$00,$98,$21,$98,$98,$98 . . .
SFX_Fail2:         .byte $0E,$EE,$00,$AC,$81,$AC,$21,$AB . . .
. . .
```

The LIBSOUND_PLAYSFX_AA library macro is called to play the sound effects in game.

gamePlayer.asm

```
// Play the sfx
LIBSOUND_PLAYSFX_AA(gameDataSID, SFX_Crab)
```

It is possible to manually create and play SID sound effects but as the beach bar game doesn't use this method it's suggested to refer to the RetroGameDev C64 Edition Volume 1 book to investigate further.

- Press **F6** to assemble and run in the VICE emulator.

The background music now plays and sound effects play for various in game events.

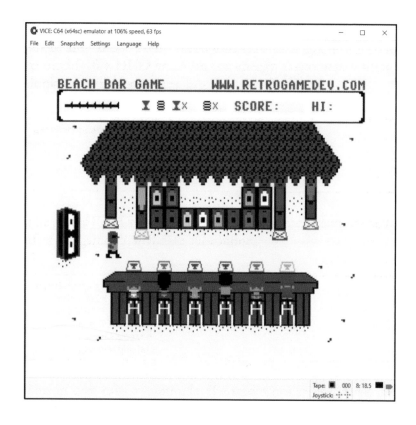

Try changing the background music

Try attaching the sound effects to different game events

Chapter 13: That's a Wrap

- Open **Ch13.code-workspace** in **Visual Studio Code**.

Gameflow

There are 2 gameflow states implemented with a jump table (the same as previous chapters).

The game starts in the menu state. When the fire button is pressed it transitions to the game state. When the energy reaches zero, it returns to the menu state.

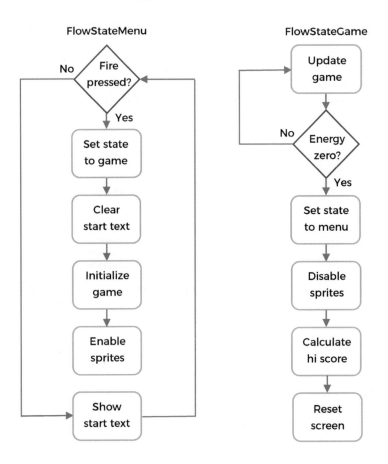

HUD

The HUD (Heads Up Display) panel is used to give feedback on the current state of the game.

There are various HUD subroutine calls throughout the code to modify the HUD variables for energy, customers waiting, drinks, towels, and scores. E.g.

gameBar.asm

```
gameBarUpdateStateWaiting:
    . . .
    // Lose some Energy
    jsr gameHUDDecreaseEnergy
    . . .
```

The gameHUDUpdate subroutine is called each frame directly after the gameFlowUpdate subroutine.

gameMain.asm

```
gameMainUpdate:
    LIBSCREEN_WAIT_V(250)    // Wait for scanline 250
    LIBSPRITE_UPDATE()       // Update the sprites
    jsr gameFlowUpdate       // Update the game flow subroutines
    jsr gameHUDUpdate        // Update the HUD subroutines
    jmp gameMainUpdate       // Jump back, infinite loop
```

This in turn calls a multitude of subroutines to update all the individual HUD elements on the HUD panel.

gameHUD.asm

```
gameHUDUpdate:
    jsr gameHUDUpdateEnergy
    jsr gameHUDUpdateBarCustomers
    jsr gameHUDUpdateLoungersCustomers
    jsr gameHUDUpdateNumDrinks
    jsr gameHUDUpdateNumTowels
    jsr gameHUDUpdateDrinksCarrying
    jsr gameHUDUpdateScore
    jsr gameHUDUpdateHiScore
    rts
```

The Energy, BarCustomers, and LoungersCustomers updates use the LIBSCREEN_SETCOLOR macros to change the color of a specific character on the HUD panel.

gameHUD.asm

```
gameHUDUpdateBarCustomers:
    lda bHudBarCustomers // Load number of bar customers
    bne gHUBCRed // If not 0, skip to red
    // Set icon to green
    LIBSCREEN_SETCOLOR_S_VVV(HUDBarCustomersColumn,HUDRow, GRE
EN)
    jmp gHUBCEnd // Skip to end
gHUBCRed:
    // Set icon to red
    LIBSCREEN_SETCOLOR_S_VVV(HUDBarCustomersColumn,HUDRow, RED)
gHUBCEnd:
    rts
```

The NumDrinks and NumTowels updates convert the specific HUD variable to ASCII to look up the digit from the character set with LIBSCREEN_SETCHARACTER macro.

gameHUD.asm

```
gameHUDUpdateNumDrinks:
    lda bHudNumDrinks
    ora #$30              // Convert to ascii
    sta ZeroPage9
    LIBSCREEN_SETCHARACTER_S_VVA(HUDNumDrinksColumn, HUDRow, Z
eroPage9)
    rts
```

The scores are more complex because we require more than 1 digit in the HUD panel and it's processor intensive to extract individual decimal digits from a variable.

The solution to this is to use the built in Decimal Mode of the 6510 when we increment the score which has the effect of storing each digit as 0-9 in an easy format for display.

gameHUD.asm

```
gameHUDIncreaseScore:
    sed // Set decimal mode
    LIBMATH_ADD16BIT_AVA(wHudScore,HUDScoreIncrease,wHudScore)
    cld // Clear decimal mode
    rts
```

The scores are stored in a word (in decimal format), then extracted for display by taking 2 digits from the low byte (4 bits per digit) and 1 digit from the high byte.

gameHUD.asm

```
gameHUDUpdateScore:
    // -------- 1st digit --------
    lda wHudScore+1

    // get low nibble
    and #%00001111

    // convert to ascii
    ora #$30
    sta ZeroPage9

    LIBSCREEN_SETCHARACTER_S_VVA(HUDScoreColumn1, HUDRow, Zero
Page9)

    // -------- 2nd digit --------
    lda wHudScore

    // get high nibble
    and #%11110000

    // convert to ascii
    lsr
    lsr
    lsr
    lsr
    ora #$30
    sta ZeroPage9

    LIBSCREEN_SETCHARACTER_S_VVA(HUDScoreColumn2, HUDRow, Zero
Page9)

    // -------- 3rd digit --------
    lda wHudScore

    // get low nibble
    and #%00001111

    // convert to ascii
    ora #$30
    sta ZeroPage9

    LIBSCREEN_SETCHARACTER_S_VVA(HUDScoreColumn3, HUDRow, Zero
Page9)

    rts
```

Memory Usage

64K

Code 6.6K

Screens 4.2K

Sprites 2.1K

Characters 2K

Sounds 2.4K

0K

Kick Assembler Build
OUTPUT

```
Memory Map
----------
Default-segment:
    $0801-$080d Basic Loader
    $1000-$19bf Sounds
    $2000-$27ff Characters
    $2800-$307f Sprites
    $3080-$411f Screens
    $4120-$5b97 Code
```

Memory sizes

BASIC Loader: 13 bytes
Sounds: 2496 bytes
Characters: 2048 bytes (256 characters)
Sprites: 2176 bytes (34 sprites)
Screens: 4256 bytes (4 screens)
Code: 6776 bytes
Total: 17765 bytes (17.3K)
Prg Size: 20.8K (due to gaps)

The Noice Kick Assembler memory viewer can be used to display memory visually.

Paste the contents of the Kick Assembler Build OUTPUT window into the memory map window at kickassmemoryview.insoft.se.

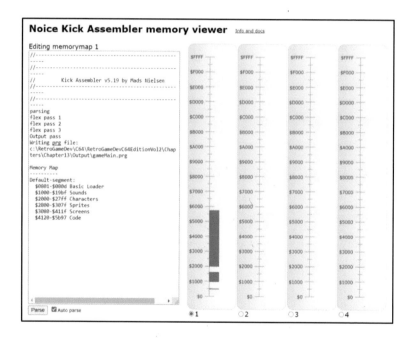

And that brings us to the end of our journey, although you could take the development further. Some ideas to get you started are a title screen, more music, save/load high scores, and animated background graphics (such as the sea).

Enjoy!

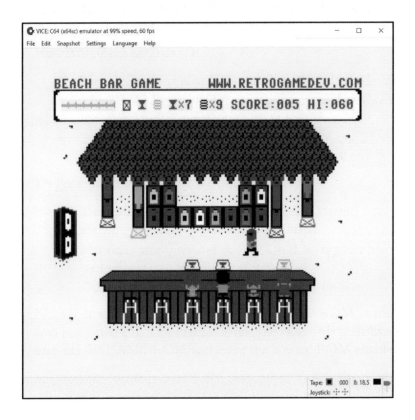

Try modding the game and posting to retrogamedev.com/forum

PART III: REFERENCE

Chapter 14: Library Code

As with the first volume it has been decided to provide the library code as a set of macros rather than subroutines, even though subroutines can provide a smaller memory footprint in certain use cases.

The main reasons were:

- When including the library code, only the macros used take up memory, whereas one copy of each subroutine would be assembled even if not used.
- Subroutines have a speed disadvantage of the extra **jsr** and **rts** instructions.
- With run-time loops (not Kick Assembler build-time loops) it's more memory efficient to use a macro without the **jsr** and **rts** as macros are only placed into memory once in this instance.
- Macros can have parameters passed in.

However, if the memory space saving of subroutines is required, it's trivial to convert a macro to a subroutine or wrapped subroutine (See Chapter 2: Key Concepts – Macros and Subroutines)

Also see the example wrapped subroutine code for:

LIBSCREEN_SETCHARACTER_S.
LIBSCREEN_SETCOLOR_S.

In addition to the following library code reference, it can be useful to study the reference books found in the Credits section.

libInput

LIBINPUT_GET_V(bPortMask)

Parameters:
bPortMask: Bitmask for required direction or fire.

Notes:
Loads the joystick state, then masks with bPortMask. Test with bne after call which will branch if not pressed (Zero Flag not 0).
CIAPRA = joystick 2, CIAPRB = joystick 1.

Mapping the Commodore 64 pages:
176, 177.

Parameter variants:
None.

==

libMath

LIBMATH_8BITTOBCD_AA(bIn, wOut)

Parameters:
bIn: Byte to convert.
wOut: BCD converted word.

Notes:
Converts a byte to a BCD (Binary Coded Decimal) word for easy display.
See 6502.org/source/integers/hex2dec-more.htm for more explanation.

Mapping the Commodore 64 pages:
None.

Parameter variants:
None.

LIBMATH_16BITTOBCD_AAA(wIn, wOut, bOut)

Parameters:
wIn: Word to convert.
wOut: BCD converted word.
bOut: BCD converted extra byte.

Notes:
Converts a word to a BCD (Binary Coded Decimal) word and byte for easy display. See 6502.org/source/integers/hex2dec-more.htm for more explanation.

Mapping the Commodore 64 pages:
None.

Parameter variants:
None.

========================

LIBMATH_ADD8BIT_AAA(bNum1, bNum2, bSum)

Parameters:
bNum1: First byte to add.
bNum2: Second byte to add.
bSum: Result of bNum1 + bNum2.

Notes:
Uses adc (ADd to accumulator with Carry) to add bNum1 + bNum2 + Carry Flag. Using the Carry Flag allows for additions to be chained, therefore the Carry Flag needs to be cleared before the first addition.

Mapping the Commodore 64 pages:
None.

Parameter variants:
LIBMATH_ADD8BIT_AVA.

LIBMATH_ADD16BIT_AVA(wNum1, wNum2, wSum)

Parameters:
wNum1: First word to add.
wNum2: Second word to add.
wSum: Result of wNum1 + wNum2.

Notes:
The same as LIBMATH_ADD8BIT but operates on the low byte followed by the high byte. The Carry Flag only needs to be cleared before the first addition.

Mapping the Commodore 64 pages:
None.

Parameter variants:
None.

======================================

LIBMATH_GREATEREQUAL8BIT_AA(bNum1, bNum2)

Parameters:
bNum1: First byte to compare.
bNum2: Second byte to compare.

Notes:
Compares the second number to the first using the cmp instruction which modifies the The Carry Flag. Test with bcc after call which will branch if the Carry Flag is 0.

Mapping the Commodore 64 pages:
None.

Parameter variants:
None.

LIBMATH_MAX8BIT_AV(bNum1, bNum2)

Parameters:
bNum1: First byte to compare / Max result.
bNum2: Second byte to compare.

Notes:
Compares the first number to the second using the cmp instruction which modifies the Carry Flag. The bcc instruction checks the Carry Flag to either skip or replace bNum1 with bNum2.

Mapping the Commodore 64 pages:
None.

Parameter variants:
None.

========================

LIBMATH_MAX16BIT_AV(wNum1, wNum2)

Parameters:
wNum1: First word to compare / Max result.
wNum2: Second word to compare.

Notes:
The same as LIBMATH_MAX8BIT but operates on the high byte followed by the low byte.

Mapping the Commodore 64 pages:
None.

Parameter variants:
None.

LIBMATH_MIN8BIT_AV(bNum1, bNum2)

Parameters:
bNum1: First byte to compare / Min result.
bNum2: Second byte to compare.

Notes:
Compares the first number to the second using the cmp instruction which modifies the Carry Flag. The bcs instruction checks the Carry Flag to either skip or replace bNum1 with bNum2.

Mapping the Commodore 64 pages:
None.

Parameter variants:
None.

=========================

LIBMATH_MIN16BIT_AV(wNum1, wNum2)

Parameters:
wNum1: First word to compare / Min result.
wNum2: Second word to compare.

Notes:
The same as LIBMATH_MIN8BIT_AV but operates on the high byte followed by the low byte.

Mapping the Commodore 64 pages:
None.

Parameter variants:
None.

LIBMATH_RAND_AAA(bArray, bCurrent, bOut)

Parameters:
bArray: Array of random number bytes.
bCurrent: Current array index.
bOut: Returns current array value.

Notes:
Looks up into an array of MathRandomMax values using an index. The index is incremented each time and wrapped back to 0 if equal to MathRandomMax.

Mapping the Commodore 64 pages:
None.

Parameter variants:
None.

===========================

LIBMATH_RANDSEED_AA(bCurrent, bSeed)

Parameters:
bCurrent: Current array index.
bSeed: Seed value.

Notes:
Sets a new random seed (start point into the random array). Uses the and instruction to wrap the index around MathRandomMax.

Mapping the Commodore 64 pages:
None.

Parameter variants:
None.

LIBMATH_SUB8BIT_AAA(bNum1, bNum2, bSum)

Parameters:
bNum1: Byte to subtract from.
bNum2: Byte to subtract.
bSum: Result of bNum1 – bNum2.

Notes:
Uses sbc (SuBtract from accumulator with Carry) to subtract bNum1 – bNum2 – opposite of Carry Flag. Using the Carry Flag allows for subtractions to be chained, therefore the Carry Flag needs to be set before the first subtraction.

Mapping the Commodore 64 pages:
None.

Parameter variants:
LIBMATH_SUB8BIT_AVA.

========================

LIBMATH_SUB16BIT_AVA(wNum1, wNum2, wSum)

Parameters:
wNum1: Word to subtract from.
wNum2: Word to subtract.
wSum: Result of wNum1 – wNum2.

Notes:
The same as LIBMATH_SUB8BIT but operates on the low byte followed by the high byte. The Carry Flag only needs to be set before the first subtraction.

Mapping the Commodore 64 pages:
None.

Parameter variants:
None.

libRasterIRQ

Parameters:
wScanline: Display scanline to trigger interrupt.
wIrq: Interrupt routine.
bFast: Faster IRQ's? (true/false)

Notes:
Disables existing interrupts then calls LIBRASTERIRQ_SET to setup an
initial raster interrupt.

Mapping the Commodore 64 pages:
147, 183, 196.

Parameter variants:
None.

===========================

LIBRASTERIRQ_START_V(bFast)

Parameters:
bFast: Faster IRQ's? (true/false)

Notes:
Stores the A, X, and Y register values onto the stack (only if using Faster
IRQ's).

Mapping the Commodore 64 pages:
None.

Parameter variants:
None.

LIBRASTERIRQ_END_V(bFast)

Parameters:
bFast: Faster IRQ's? (true/false)

Notes:
Acknowledges the raster IRQ to the VIC-II. Then retrieves the Y, X, and A register values from the stack and returns (if using Faster IRQ's), or jumps to the default IRQ routine.

Mapping the Commodore 64 pages:
146.

Parameter variants:
None.

=========================

LIBRASTERIRQ_SET_VAV(wScanline, wIrq, bFast)

Parameters:
wScanline: Display scanline to trigger interrupt.
wIrq: Interrupt routine.
bFast: Faster IRQ's? (true/false)

Notes:
Sets the raster IRQ scanline to the VIC-II. Then sets the IRQ ROM vector (if using Faster IRQ's), or sets the IRQ RAM vector.

Mapping the Commodore 64 pages:
129, 138.

Parameter variants:
None.

libScreen

LIBSCREEN_DEBUG8BIT_VVA(bXPos, bYPos, bIn)

Parameters:
bXPos: Screen character X position (0-39).
bYPos: Screen character Y position (0-24).
bIn: Byte to display.

Notes:
Uses LIBMATH_8BITTOBCD to convert a byte to its 3 nibble (3x4 bits) BCD representation. Takes each of the 3 nibbles of the BCD number, converts them to ASCII and uses LIBSCREEN_SETCHARACTER to display.

Mapping the Commodore 64 pages:
None.

Parameter variants:
None.

========================

LIBSCREEN_DEBUG16BIT_VVA(bXPos, bYPos, wIn)

Parameters:
bXPos: Screen character X position (0-39).
bYPos: Screen character Y position (0-24).
wIn: Word to display.

Notes:
The same as LIBSCREEN_DEBUG8BIT but uses LIBMATH_16BITTOBCD to convert a word to its 5 nibble (5x4bits) BCD representation.

Mapping the Commodore 64 pages:
None.

Parameter variants:
None.

LIBSCREEN_DRAWTEXT_VVA(bXPos, bYPos, string)

Parameters:
bXPos: Screen character X position (0-39).
bYPos: Screen character Y position (0-24).
string: Zero terminated string.

Notes:
Finds the memory address of a screen character to display by looking up into the wScreenRAMRowStart array (which contains the memory addresses for the start of each row). Then loops around each character in the string (until it finds a 0) and stores the character at that address using the indirect indexed memory mode.

Mapping the Commodore 64 pages:
None.

Parameter variants:
None.

========================

LIBSCREEN_GETCHARACTER_AAA(bXPos, bYPos, bOut)

Parameters:
bXPos: Screen character X position (0-39).
bYPos: Screen character Y position (0-24).
bOut: Character value at X, Y.

Notes:
Finds the memory address of a screen character to get by looking up into the wScreenRAMRowStart array (which contains the memory addresses for the start of each row). Sets bOut to the character value at X, Y using the indirect indexed memory mode.

Mapping the Commodore 64 pages:
None.

Parameter variants:
None.

LIBSCREEN_GETCOLOR_AAA(bXPos, bYPos, bOut)

Parameters:
bXPos: Screen character X position (0-39).
bYPos: Screen character Y position (0-24).
bOut: Color value at X, Y.

Notes:
Finds the memory address of a screen color to get by looking up into the wColorRAMRowStart array (which contains the memory addresses for the start of each row). Sets bOut to the color value at X, Y using the indirect indexed memory mode. Only the lower 4 bits are used as Color RAM is only 4 bits per location.

Mapping the Commodore 64 pages:
None.

Parameter variants:
None.

===========================

LIBSCREEN_PIXELTOCHAR_AAAA(wXPixels, bYPixels, bXChar, bYChar)

Parameters:
wXPixels: Screen pixel X position (0-319).
bYPixels: Screen pixel Y position (0-199).
bXChar: Screen character X out.
bYChar: Screen character Y out.

Notes:
Divides the X and Y pixel positions by 8 to give X and Y character positions. If the X position high byte > 0 then makes an adjustment of 32 characters across (32x8 = 256).

Mapping the Commodore 64 pages:
None.

Parameter variants:
None.

LIBSCREEN_PROFILESTART()

Parameters:
None.

Notes:
Increases the border color by 1.

Mapping the Commodore 64 pages:
156.

Parameter variants:
None.

========================

LIBSCREEN_PROFILEEND()

Parameters:
None.

Notes:
Decreases the border color by 1.

Mapping the Commodore 64 pages:
156.

Parameter variants:
None.

LIBSCREEN_SETBACKGROUND_AA(wBackground, wColor)

Parameters:
wBackground: Screen character data.
wColor: Screen color data.

Notes:
Loops 250 times setting 4 blocks of screen character data to the
SCREENRAM (250 x 4 = 1000 bytes). The 1000 bytes of COLORRAM are
set by using each screen character value as a lookup into the screen
color data because there is 1 byte of color data per character (256
values), not 1 per screen location (1000). The display is disabled during
the copy to hide glitches as it takes a few frames to update.

Mapping the Commodore 64 pages:
None.

Parameter variants:
None.

========================

LIBSCREEN_SETBACKGROUNDCOLOR_V(bColor)

Parameters:
bColor: Color value.

Notes:
Sets the background color.

Mapping the Commodore 64 pages:
156.

Parameter variants:
None.

LIBSCREEN_SETBORDERCOLOR_V(bColor)

Parameters:
bColor: Color value.

Notes:
Sets the border color.

Mapping the Commodore 64 pages:
156.

Parameter variants:
None.

========================

LIBSCREEN_SETCHARACTER_S_AAA(bXPos, bYPos, bChar)

Parameters:
bXPos: Screen character X position (0-39).
bYPos: Screen character Y position (0-24).
bChar: Character value.

Notes:
Wrapped subroutine. Finds the memory address of a screen character to set by looking up into the wScreenRAMRowStart array (which contains the memory addresses for the start of each row). Sets the character value at X, Y to bChar using the indirect indexed memory mode.

Mapping the Commodore 64 pages:
None.

Parameter variants:
LIBSCREEN_SETCHARACTER_S_AAA
LIBSCREEN_SETCHARACTER_S_AAV
LIBSCREEN_SETCHARACTER_S_VVA

LIBSCREEN_SETCHARMEMORY_V(bCharSlot)

Parameters:
bCharSlot: Character set memory slot.

Notes:
Sets the required character set memory slot to the VIC-II. (See the
Character Memory section on **page 103** in the **C64 Programmer's
Reference Guide** for more information on character set memory
locations).

Mapping the Commodore 64 pages:
145.

Parameter variants:
None.

=========================

LIBSCREEN_SETCOLOR_S_AAA(bXPos, bYPos, bColor)

Parameters:
bXPos: Screen character X position (0-39).
bYPos: Screen character Y position (0-24).
bColor: Color value.

Notes:
Wrapped subroutine. Finds the memory address of a screen color to set
by looking up into the wColorRAMRowStart array (which contains the
memory addresses for the start of each row). Sets the color value at X, Y
to bColor using the indirect indexed memory mode.

Mapping the Commodore 64 pages:
None.

Parameter variants:
LIBSCREEN_SETCOLOR_S_AAA
LIBSCREEN_SETCOLOR_S_AVV
LIBSCREEN_SETCOLOR_S_VVA
LIBSCREEN_SETCOLOR_S_VVV

LIBSCREEN_SETDISPLAYENABLE_V(bEnable)

Parameters:
bEnable: Display enabled? (true/false)

Notes:
Enables or disables the VIC-II screen display.

Mapping the Commodore 64 pages:
129.

Parameter variants:
None.

=========================

LIBSCREEN_SETMULTICOLORMODE_V(bEnable)

Parameters:
bEnable: Multicolor enabled? (true/false)

Notes:
Enables or disables multicolor screen mode.

Mapping the Commodore 64 pages:
140.

Parameter variants:
None.

LIBSCREEN_SETMULTICOLORS_VV(bColor1, bColor2)

Parameters:
bColor1: Color value 1.
bColor2: Color value 2.

Notes:
Sets the 2 screen multicolors.

Mapping the Commodore 64 pages:
156.

Parameter variants:
None.

========================

LIBSCREEN_SETSCREENCOLOR_V(bColor)

Parameters:
bColor: Color value.

Notes:
Sets the border color and background color.

Mapping the Commodore 64 pages:
156.

Parameter variants:
None.

LIBSCREEN_WAIT_V(wScanline)

Parameters:
wScanline: Display scanline to wait for.

Notes:
Stalls in a loop until the desired scanline is reached.

Mapping the Commodore 64 pages:
129, 138.

Parameter variants:
None.

libSound

Parameters:
wSidfile: SID music/sfx data.

Notes:
Finds out if the current C64 is PAL. Calls the SID initialize routine.

Mapping the Commodore 64 pages:
None.

Parameter variants:
None.

=========================

LIBSOUND_PLAYSFX_AA(wSidfile, wSound)

Parameters:
wSidfile: SID music/sfx data.
wSound: Sfx byte array.

Notes:
Calls the SID sfx play routine with the specified sfx data.

Mapping the Commodore 64 pages:
None.

Parameter variants:
None.

LIBSOUND_UPDATE_A(wSidfile)

Parameters:
wSidfile: SID music/sfx data.

Notes:
Calls the SID update routine. Skip some updates if C64 is NTSC to slow down to the same speed as PAL. This routine is designed to play PAL SID files on PAL and NTSC.

Mapping the Commodore 64 pages:
None.

Parameter variants:
None.

libSprite

LIBSPRITE_DIDCOLLIDESP_A(bSprite)

Parameters:
bSprite: Sprite number.

Notes:
Masks the sprite the sprite collision register against the
spriteNumberMask. Test with beq after call which will branch if no
collision occurred (Zero Flag is 1).

Mapping the Commodore 64 pages:
155.

Parameter variants:
None.

=========================

LIBSPRITE_ENABLE_AV(bSprite, bEnable)

Parameters:
bSprite: Sprite number.
bEnable: Sprite enabled? (true/false)

Notes:
Enables or disables a sprite.

Mapping the Commodore 64 pages:
140.

Parameter variants:
None.

LIBSPRITE_ENABLEALL_V(bEnable)

Parameters:
bEnable: Sprites enabled? (true/false)

Notes:
Enables or disables all 8 sprites.

Mapping the Commodore 64 pages:
140.

Parameter variants:
None.

=========================

LIBSPRITE_MULTICOLORENABLEALL_V(bEnable)

Parameters:
bEnable: Multicolor enabled? (true/false)

Notes:
Enables or disables multicolor sprite mode.

Mapping the Commodore 64 pages:
153.

Parameter variants:
None.

LIBSPRITE_PLAYANIM_AAAVV(bSprite, bStartFrame, bEndFrame, bSpeed, bLoop)

Parameters:
bSprite: Sprite number.
bStartFrame: Start frame number.
bEndFrame: End frame number.
bSpeed: Frames to skip before updating.
bLoop: Continue animating? (true/false)

Notes:
If the sprite is active and either the start or end frame numbers have changed then update all of the sprite array values.

Mapping the Commodore 64 pages:
None.

Parameter variants:
LIBSPRITE_PLAYANIM_AVVVV

==========================

LIBSPRITE_SETCOLOR_AA(bSprite, bColor)

Parameters:
bSprite: Sprite number.
bColor: Color value.

Notes:
Sets the sprite color VIC-II register.

Mapping the Commodore 64 pages:
157.

Parameter variants:
LIBSPRITE_SETCOLOR_AV
LIBSPRITE_SETCOLOR_VV

LIBSPRITE_SETALLCOLORS_V(bColor)

Parameters:
bColor: Color value.

Notes:
Sets all 8 sprite color VIC-II registers.

Mapping the Commodore 64 pages:
157.

Parameter variants:
None.

=========================

LIBSPRITE_SETFRAME_AA(bSprite, bIndex)

Parameters:
bSprite: Sprite number.
bIndex: Frame index.

Notes:
Stops any existing animation for the sprite. Sets the sprite RAM pointer to bIndex + SPRITERAM. (See the **Sprite Pointers** section on **page 133** in the **C64 Programmer's Reference Guide** for more information on sprite memory locations).

Mapping the Commodore 64 pages:
None.

Parameter variants:
LIBSPRITE_SETFRAME_AV
LIBSPRITE_SETFRAME_VV

LIBSPRITE_SETMULTICOLORS_VV(bColor1, bColor2)

Parameters:
bColor1: Color value 1.
bColor2: Color value 2.

Notes:
Sets the 2 sprite multicolors.

Mapping the Commodore 64 pages:
157.

Parameter variants:
None.

=========================

LIBSPRITE_SETPOSITION_AAA(bSprite, wXPos, bYPos)

Parameters:
bSprite: Sprite number.
wXPos: Screen pixel X position.
bYPos: Screen pixel Y position.

Notes:
Sets the sprite X low, X high, and Y position VIC-II registers. Note that the X low and Y registers are interleaved in memory (i.e. SP0X, SP0Y, SP1X, SP1Y, ... etc.).

Mapping the Commodore 64 pages:
127, 128.

Parameter variants:
LIBSPRITE_SETPOSITION_AAV
LIBSPRITE_SETPOSITION_VAV

LIBSPRITE_STOPANIM_A(bSprite)

Parameters:
bSprite: Sprite number.

Notes:
Stops any existing animation for the sprite.

Mapping the Commodore 64 pages:
None.

Parameter variants:
None.

==========================

LIBSPRITE_UPDATE()

Parameters:
None.

Notes:
Runs through each sprite's arrays and updates the current animation frame if the delay has reached 0. Disables the sprite if inactive. (See the **Sprite Pointers** section on **page 133** in the **C64 Programmer's Reference Guide** for more information on sprite memory locations).

Mapping the Commodore 64 pages:
None.

Parameter variants:
None.

libUtility

LIBUTILITY_DISABLEBASIC()

Parameters:
None.

Notes:
Swaps out the BASIC ROM for RAM.

Mapping the Commodore 64 pages:
4.

Parameter variants:
None.

============================

LIBUTILITY_DISABLEBASICANDKERNAL()

Parameters:
None.

Notes:
Swaps out the BASIC and Kernal ROMs for RAM. Calls
LIBUTILITY_DISABLENMI to disable NMI interrupts.

Mapping the Commodore 64 pages:
4, 183, 196.

Parameter variants:
None.

LIBUTILITY_DISABLENMI()

Parameters:
None.

Notes:
Disables NMI interrupts. This has the effect of stopping the Run/Stop &
Restore key combination from halting the program.

Mapping the Commodore 64 pages:
None.

Parameter variants:
None.

========================

LIBUTILITY_SET1000_AV(wStart, bValue)

Parameters:
wStart: Start memory location.
bValue: Value to set.

Notes:
Loops 250 times setting 4 blocks of memory to bValue (250 x 4 = 1000
bytes).

Mapping the Commodore 64 pages:
None.

Parameter variants:
None.

LIBUTILITY_WAITLOOP_V(bNumLoops)

Parameters:
bNumLoops: Number of loops to wait.

Notes:
Loops around bNumLoops times.

Mapping the Commodore 64 pages:
None.

Parameter variants:
None.

Credits

Cover Art:

Rick Nath

Andy Jackson

surface3d.co.uk

Music and Sfx:

Andrzej Kucharski (Akadem)

bit.ly/3cnVuIr

Kamil Degorski (Djinn)

bit.ly/3iXdPO0

Richard/TND

tnd64.unikat.sk

Tools:

Oracle Java

java.com

Microsoft Visual Studio Code

code.visualstudio.com

Kick Assembler – Mads Nielsen

theweb.dk/KickAssembler

Kick Assembler extension - Paul Hocker

bit.ly/36iiLYE

C64 Debugger - slajerek

sourceforge.net/projects/c64-debugger

C64 Debug GUI - stigzler

magoarcade.org/wp/c64debuggui

VICE Emulator

vice-emu.sourceforge.io

CharPad / SpritePad – Subchrist Software

subchristsoftware.com

GoatTracker 2 – jauernig, loorni

sourceforge.net/projects/goattracker2

Noice Memory Viewer – Swoffa, Bernie

kickassmemoryview.insoft.se

Reference Books:

Commodore 64 Programmer's Reference Guide
Commodore Business Machines, Inc.

Mapping the Commodore 64
Sheldon Leemon

Assembly Language Programming with the C64
Marvin L. De Jong

Assembly in One Step
David A. Wheeler

Special Thanks:

John Dale (OldSkoolCoder)

oldskoolcoder.co.uk

youtube.com/c/OldSkoolCoder

Glenn Cline (GRay Defender)

graydefender.com

youtube.com/c/GRayDefender

Michal Taszycki

64bites.com

Andrew Jacobs

obelisk.me.uk

Printed in Great Britain
by Amazon

53231663R00087